UPANISHADS
AND
ISLAMIC MYSTICISM

UPANISHADS AND ISLAMIC MYSTICISM

Dr. Intaj Malek

BKP

BHARATIYA KALA PRAKASHAN

DELHI (INDIA)

First Published : 2004

ISBN : 81-8090-064-9

Published by	: **C.P. Gautam** *for* **BHARATIYA KALA PRAKASHAN** 3421-A, IInd Floor, Narang Colony, Tri Nagar, Delhi-110035. Phone : 27393083, 30967505 (O) 27522129 (R)
Laser Typesetting by	: Twinkle Graphics, Delhi-110085.
Printed by	: BDH Printer at Salasar Imaging Systems Delhi-35. Ph : 31045804

Dedicated to the fountain of inspiration

Dr. Yajneshwar Shastri

Dr. Sunanda Shastri

Prof. B.M. Peerzada

and

My daughter Falak to get inspiration

Contents

Foreword

It gives me great pleasure in writing a few words of introduction to 'Upanishads and Islamic Mysticism' by Dr. Intaj Malek. The title of the monograph itself reveals the special contribution made by the author to the field of knowledge, particularly to the field of Philosophy. This kind of comparative study on Upanishadic and Islamic Mysticism is first of its kind. Dr. Malek's treatment of subject matter is exhaustive and extremely well written.

The study of Philosophy is a rigorous study and to write on comparative study on completely two diverse philosophy of Mysticism is rather more rigorous. Dr. Malek has taken a great pain in comparing these two diverse currents ultimately leading to the same goal. It is rightly said in this small monograph that Indian philosophy and particularly Upanishadic Philosophy has spread the aroma of love and brotherhood all over the world. The Vedas and the Upanishads have provided the world the right understanding and the right knowledge. In fact they have provided the world the right way of living. Indeed they are proud possessions of our glorious past.

The Upanishads are full of mystical mantras. The *'Isha'* Upanishad's first stanza is full of the mystery of the cosmos. Dr. Malek while writing on Upanishadic and Islamic mysticism has taken into his ambiance the profuse impact of this Upanishad. He has copiously quoted from almost all Upanishads to illustrate his comparative study.

Islamic Mysticism that Dr. Malek (quoting the western scholars) calls Sufism is the heart of Islam. The real Islam lives in the life of a Sufi *Dervish.* The Sufis always talked about the unity of the Self with the Supreme Self and this is the concept hidden in the Upanishads.

This monograph contains seven chapters. Each chapter is unique in its own way. The first chapter deals with the definition of mysticism both Upanishadic and Islamic. It presents beautifully the origin and evolution as well as the comparative definitions and meaning of Mysticism. The chapter that follows vividly presents deep understanding of the *Tasawwuf* the Islamic Mysticism, its characteristics and its main concepts and fundamentals. Dr. Malek magnificently elaborates the major Sufi saints and their thoughts and the influence of Vedantins on Sufism. He has included the saints of his native place who are not yet included in the English language. Dr. Malek is not only writing on Philosophy but he is a poet and a writer and a translator. In this monograph he has translated some couplets from the well-known Gujarati Sufi mystic *Anwar Kazi's* work *Gulshane Khusi* previously known as *Anwar Bhajnavali.* The poet mystic Anwar Kazi was a great Sufi saint who lived a life with very meager worldly things. He had written *Bhajans* addressing the Lord as Hari and Krishna. He was a great Sufi of Gujarat who mingled in his work the unity of two diverse cultures i.e. Hindu- Muslim culture. Another great names in Sufism are Hallaj Mansoor and Mawlana Jalaluddin Rumi. Rumi is most widely read and translated Sufi mystic. Rumi's Mathnavi and Songs in praise of Shams of Tabriz are so well known that they hardly need any more elaboration here in the foreword. Dr. Intaj Malek has copiously quoted from Rumi the mystic Sufi that gives a special flavour to his monograph.

The monographic work in its own is beautifully written which will be helpful to all who love philosophy and religious and cultural studies. I have no hesitation in recommendating this work to the readers of philosophy and comparative religions. I am sure it will get the due welcome, which it deserves. I personally look forward to many more such works by this young scholar.

Ahmedabad
1st May 2004

Prof. Dr. Yajneshwar Shastri
Director
University School of Psychology,
Education and Philosophy
Gujarat University, Ahmedabad

Preface

Mysticism has always remained a cynosure for me since my childhood days but my dream to understand the term in its complexity, simplicity, and beauty came true when I decided to write on Mysticism.

Upanishads and Islamic Mysticism is the subject that has enhanced the appetite of my soul.

Needless to narrate the beauty of the Upanishads here in the preface but I cannot prevent my self from saying that the Upanishads do have everything that can satisfy the spiritual appetite of human beings. They are full of poetic beauty; spirituality and morality accompanied by an emphasis on knowledge of the Self that is Brahman. Upanishads are a proud possession of the Indian mystical tradition that has opened the new horizons for the development of other mystical traditions. Whether the western scholars agree or not the Upanishads are the roots of the mystical traditions evolved in the world.

Islamic Mysticism that is popularly or rather fondly known as Sufism seems to me very similar to the Upanishadic mysticism. The Sufi mystics of Islam do talk about the unity of the Self with the Supreme self i.e. the Brahman in Upanishadic language. I have allotted, two separate chapters to the discussion of mysticism of the Upanishads as well as to the discussion of Taswwuf (Islamic mysticism or Sufism). I have tried to bring out the conclusion that the ultimate Reality remains one and the same by a comparative study of both of these mystical traditions. I have also assigned a separate place in the form of a chapter to Sufi saints and mystics and their mystical thoughts and also the influence of the Vedantins on them.

India is a beautiful garden with varied religious flowers and plants spreading to the world the aroma of love and brotherhood, peace and non violence, kindness and generosity not only towards human beings but towards animals and to the vegetation world. It is in such a garden that the flowers of Upanishads blossomed and ripened into fruits giving nectar to the entire world. It is because of these magnanimity and richness of spirituality that encouraged me to write on such a subject.

My monograph will be beneficial to the students, scholars, teachers, research workers and to the people *enmasse* who are interested in the study of mysticism and to those who want to bridge the gap among people of different sects adhering to different religions.

I regret my inability, as I could not use diacritical marks for Sanskrit terms and transliteration used in this study due to some technical reasons. I have used Arabic Sufistic terms in many places for that I have given an exhaustive glossary.

Dr. Yajneshwar Shastri has always remained a source of inspiration. I am highly thankful to him for his generous help without caring for time, and writing a foreword to this book. I owe my thanks and gratitude to Dr. Sunanda Shastri as she has always encouraged me with her suggestions and Mr. Yogesh Shastri for his kind help to do proof reading. Special thanks to my cousin M. Bakar Momin and Mr. Jagadish Shah who helped me to prepare footnotes and bibliography. I would like to thank my wife Mumtaz Malek who has always been helpful to me in making the reference materials ready whenever I needed them. How can I forget Principal Mr. B M Peerzada *ex.* Dean of the Gujarat University who is a fountain of inspiration, a living legend and a personality larger than life? I also thank Mr. C.P. Gautam of Bharatiya Kala Prakashan Delhi for beautifully designing and printing my work in a book form.

Ahmedabad **Dr. INTAJ MALEK**
1st June 2004

Chapter 1

Introduction to Mysticism–Upanishadic and Islamic

The term "mysticism" comes from the classical Greco-Roman mystery cults. Perhaps it came from *myein* meaning "to close the lips and eyes, and refers to the sacred oath of the initiates, the *mystes*, to keep secret about the inner workings of the religion." In Neo-Platonism "mysticism" came to be associated with secrecy of any kind. The term *mystica* appeared in the Christian treatise, *Mystica Theologia,* of an anonymous Syrian Neoplatonist monk of the late fifth or early sixth century, who was known pseudonymously as Dionysius the Areopagite. In this work mysticism was described as the secrecy of the mind.

Despite the various approaches to mysticism it seems to possess some common characteristics. Such were the findings of the philosopher W.T. Stace, who discovered seven common themes of mysticism when studying Roman Catholic, Protestant, ancient classical, Hindu, and American agnostic mystical experiences. They were (1) a unifying vision and perception of the one by the senses and through many objects; (2) the apprehension of the one as an inner life; (3) objective and true sense of reality; (4) feelings of satisfaction, joy, and bliss; (5) a religious element that is a feeling of the holy and sacred; (6) a paradoxical feeling; (7) and inexpressible feelings.

According to mystic philosophy, one cannot gain a full understanding of God, the nature of the universe, or indeed the 'Self', by external or physical means alone, because God, religion and spirituality all exist within our own selves, within our own souls.

By 'closing the eyes' and shutting out the external physical world of the five senses through introspection, meditation or prayer, a divine union with God, can be experienced by the individual. Meditation, introspection and prayer are common to all religions, and yet mysticism is not a religion because it has no hierarchy, no rules, no regulations, and no sacred scriptures. In mysticism the central character is Self and you are, in your highest sense, both the worshipped and the worshiper, both temple and congregation.

The mystical journey is, by its very nature, a journey into the self, and a journey ultimately made alone. The mystical and supernatural however, may also be experienced spontaneously by those with no religious ritualistic affiliations. It can be experienced even by atheists and agnostics alike. Apparently regardless of all belief and outward form, the mystical experience appears to exist and function as an internal vision or realization within the 'soul' or the self, and not as an externalised sensual experience.

The mystic tradition itself pre-dates organised religion and is ultimately the very foundation of all religions, whether they are pagan, primal or otherwise and mystical revelation can be clearly seen to be at the heart of them all. This includes the Eastern philosophies of Hinduism and Buddhism as well as the three Western monotheistic religions, Judaism, Christianity and Islam, the latter of which were founded on the mystical revelations of their own respective teachers or prophets, Buddha, Moses, Jesus Christ and Mohammed.[1] ﷺ

Although the three great monotheistic religions which originated in the Middle, East–Judaism, Christianity and islam–are based on the individual vision, revelation, and mystical experience of these divine messengers or prophets.

Mysticism or the search for the veiled truth that pervades the fabric of nature is aroused by the mysterious projection of the universe. It is a labyrinth where lovers are lost and the real pleasure of existence lies in search for the beloved, which grows deeper and more interesting with rising hope and intensified desire.

It is always for the lover to look for the beloved and do all the wooing. When a beloved becomes a wooer, he or she loses the status of the beloved. The true zest of love lies in the search which multiplies with the degree of sincerity, sobriety and strain involved in the exploration. Those who have had an experience of true love, know the value of sighs, sorrows and supplications suffused with selflessness, no matter how suffocating, suppressing and stifling the experience turns out to be.

In the world of mysticism, it is the language of love that prevails, irrespective of, whether we indulge in the Indian Christian or Islamic mysticism. It is poetic in nature and packed with an emotional appeal bursting with desire. In reality it is pure and perfect carrying the pomp and prestige of ardent love which is original, innocent and overwhelming. When we apply this to the origin of mysticism, India stands out as the true home of mysticism because in the Vedas, the Indian scriptures, it is man who woos God being inspired by the fear, reverence and wonder of nature. The other religions such as Judaism, Christianity and Islam have exactly the opposite approach. In these faiths, it is God who contacts man. An Indian mystic believes that the natural phenomenon *i.e.*, the world of appearance is a veil between the Reality and man, the seeker, who must initiate a probe for Brahman, the Reality, and he can trace Him through acquired and intuitive knowledge only. On the contrary, the Sematic religions hold that it is God who reveals Himself to man because He wants to be worshipped and desires to guide man; people who believe in Him are guided and saved. But the unbelievers are thrown into hell. This philosophy clearly shows that :

a. Relationship between God and man is not that of love because he forces himself on man through revelation.

b. Man is not a lover but a slave who is required by divine command to obey and worship the Almighty.

c. The fact that God reveals Himself and does not observe a veil cheapens Himself and thus divests Himself of the adoration that true love deserves.

d. Again, as God destroys those who do not worship Him, the entire purpose of revelation and creation is the glorification of god, and man becomes just a pawn in the phenomenal game.

This is self explanatory from the following quotations :

1. Exodus 3:4 clearly states about Moses that an angel of God appeared before him from a burning bush. It was an act of God's revelation, and He wanted to impress man (Moses) with His Divine power. Therefore, though the bush burnt, it was not consumed.[2]

Exodus 4 : 10-14 narrates yet another episode which states that Moses was reluctant to carry the burden of prophet hood owing to being non-eloquent, because of his defective speech. God argues with him to accept the responsibility as a prophet : "Now, therefore go, and I will be with thy mouth, and teach thee what thou shalt say." But when Moses still dithers, he does so at the risk of kindling God's wrath!

2. Though there is no mention of Trinity in the New Testament, this happens to be the basic belief of the Christians. Most Christians believe in Jesus not as God, the Son, but as God incarnate, meaning that he was God in the form of man.

The mere fact of his birth, growing and preaching constitutes an act of revelation. The desire of Jesus to be acknowledged as God was so strong that he was crucified on the charge of blasphemy though the faithful put on it an entirely different interpretation, which seeks to portray it as an act of salvation for the human race.

Jesus wanted to be loved by mankind; like Yahweh, the Jewish God, he appears as a jealous God because he does not like the idea of people loving anybody else including one's father, mother, sons and daughters.[3] In fact he goes even further, and demands that one must prove one's love for him by hating one's father, mother, wife, children, brothers, sisters and even one's life.

It is rather strange; love is a natural trait and function of the lover, if he/she does not show an intense desire for the beloved voluntarily, one can assume with certainty that there is no spark of affection. Of course; it is unnatural, and even vulgar, to demand to be treated as a beloved along with the compliments that a true love deserves. Once God has revealed Himself, He has lost the status of a beloved. In fact, revelation is an act of a beloved chasing the 'lover." I need not say what people think of such a beloved.

3. Orthodox Islam also advocates the same divine approach, which clearly shows that God imposes Himself on man through revelation. There is an event in the life of the Prophet Muhamad, which has not been challenged by anyone in the Muslim world. It states that, according to Muhammad, the Word of God was revealed to him by the Archangel Gabriel. This luminous figure caught him by the throat and commanded him to repeat the sacred words but he tried to flee. Muhammad suspected the genuineness of his message and was afraid that the revelation resembled the claims of the visionary poets of his time who frequented the streets of Mecca with their pretence of being divinely illuminated.

There came to him (Muhammad) the angel and said : Recite, to which he replied, I am not lettered. He took hold of me (the apostle said) and pressed me, until I was hard-pressed; thereafter, he let me off and said : Recite, to which I replied, I am not lettered. He took hold of me and pressed me for the third time, till I was hard pressed and then let me go and said : Recite in the name of your Lord who created you from a clot of blood. Recite. And your most bountiful Lord is He who taught the use of pen–taught what you knew not. Then the Prophet returned therewith, his heart was trembling, and he went to Khadija and said : Wrap me up, wrap me up. So they wrapped him till the fear had left him. This is the first mystical experience encountered by the prophet. The orthodox Islam talks about such commanding Religion, Sufism is totally different from such commanding Religion. Mysticism is a love affair that only Yogis and Sufi mystics do afford. The Shari'a people who pretend to be true Islamic in fact lack the spirit of Islam. True Islam does not lie in the religious rituals and five time prostration and adopting following the command of the master that is Allah. The core of Islam lies into Sufism. Sufism is neither a deviant path nor a pseudo Islamic path. They are neither idolaters nor iconoclasts they are rather the lovers of god. God is their beloved (Dulhan) and they are the grooms or in certain cases they are the Dulhans (brides) of God. This love affair between the seen and the unseen, between the man and God, between matter and spirit is called mysticism. Thousands of Sufis from time immemorial have been practicing this love affair and they have been relentlessly trying to reveal the beauty of Allah in its totality, nudity and magnanimity before humanity. They have never afraid of what their future would be. Many met with their tragic death for revealing the truth only because it was sin in the eyes of Shari'a. The love affair of the Sufis become real Tawhid when they recite or chant La-ilaha IL-Lillah on and on in a prescribed adab. Some Majdhubs tie themselves hanging down their heads into the well for days and nights together chanting the mantra

ALLAHOO...either ALLAHOO or LAILAH IL-ALLAH or ALHMDU LILLAH or ALLAHU AKBAR or ISHQ ALLAH, MA'BUD LILLAH. This is their love affair with God the unseen. Here we find the influence of the Hath yogis on Sufi mystics. Here the chanting of any particular mantra or making any particular sound is not important what is more important is their oneness with the ultimate Reality. They become Fana-Fi llah, fana in the path of love with God.

4. Though the Vedas are considered as the Holy Scriptures of the Hindus, I am reluctant to call them as such. To my mind, they are the sacred books of India and form an integral part of the cultural heritage of people of the Indian descent irrespective of their faith.

There are four Vedas, the oldest being the Rig-Veda, which also happens to be the root of the Vedic religion leading to its latest form known as Hinduism. The Veda is considered eternal. It is not subject to revelation; all God or Gods had to do was to promote the intuition of the pious and gifted men known as Rishis or seers who were able to see the eternal truth directly without the help of any medium including sense perception. They expressed this truth in a human language called Sanskrit.

This is the claim of the Hindu faithful, and one may be willing to admire it without acknowledging its divine origin or supernatural element. Since there is a repeated mention of the Eternal Law in the Rig-Veda, one comes to the conclusion that the Upanishadic seers were deeply interested in the natural phenomena, and thought of the universe as an organized whole. Not only the ṢAT or the systematic cosmos was governed by order and truth called ṚIT but man himself was an integral part of the universe which was likely to suffer chaos (ASAT) through the interference of the demoniac powers or antigods (ASURAS). Man had thus an obligation to make a contribution towards the maintenance of the world, and he could do so by performing sacrifices and offering Gods SOMA drink. The purpose of sacrifices, Soma and many complex rituals was to secure the propitiation of the hidden forces of nature, which influenced the quality of human life through their effect and intensity. As humans and animals have shapes and attributes which give them power to act and be nice or nasty, these forces of nature which had the ability to peel and heel, sadden and gladden and elevate and devastate, must also possess certain forms and characteristics. So, they gave these natural forces particular shapes usually human and sometimes animalist such as elephant, bull and monkey. One should also applaud the vision of the Vedic and Upanishadic man who knew that the cosmic order is hierarchical. So, they stratified these forces of nature, creating Gods and Goddesses of various ranks having different powers and prestige. The greatest of them was Dyaṣuh Pitar, Heavenly Father or the sky. Then there were Indra, the God of Indu or rain and dew, Agni, the god of fire, Surya, the Sun, Usha the goddess of the dawn, and many more. So these hidden forces ascended the human mind with mystical attributes and powers.

One ought to remember that these forces are part of the universe which is mysterious and arouses fear in man's heart. Thus, he seeks protection against this natural consternation through a set of rituals, supplications and sacrifices, which eventually emerge as a religion; it seeks to protect the human mind from fear of the cosmic vastness, mystery and uncertainty the same way as the ozone layer shields the earth from the lethal effects of the sun's ultraviolet rays. Because of its survival value, religion comes to be associated with man's instinct and almost all his actions become reflexive in relation to the next world and he usually defies reason to protect the faith, which is, in fact, a form of make-believe; he does not want to be shaken out of his daydreaming to face the Reality of life which is harsh, hazardous and even horrific, though capable of moulding into hilarity, happiness and even a halo, but it requires a lot of efforts, which he is reluctant to put in. Why? It is because religion offers him the earth just for having faith in a certain guru, prophet or messiah. Why should he suffer pain for what he calls get gratis?

Since the Veda is inspired by the mystical fear of the universe seeking peace of mind through appeasing the forces of nature including the supreme God, it represents man's spontaneous desire, and not dictated by a super-being. to mount a search for the hidden truth through meditation and rituals. This is the reason that throughout the hymns of the Rig-Veda, one cannot trace a single stanza where a god tells man to supplicate him, bow, bend or prostrate before him, worship him. Whatever rituals or forms of worship man adopts, he does so of his own free will, without any divine coercion, whatever. The Vedas, thus represent man's natural curiosity to find the Reality with a view to becoming a part of it. Of course, this situation changes with the emergence of the Orthodox Hinduism because lord Krishna wants to be worshipped by his devotees but I am concerned here with Vedas though Hinduism still preserves some of its original traits.

Since the Upanishadic quest for man of his own free will initiates Reality, it gives him the status of a lover and bestows on God the honour of being the beloved, seeking union with Him. And this has been the fundamental principle of mysticism since inception of civilization. On the contrary, the approach of the Sematic religions, as already described, is entirely the opposite; it is God who threatens man with hell or coaxes him with the offer of paradise to seek Him and thus loses the status of a beloved which constitutes the core of mysticism. This is the reason that the Biblical and Qura'nic messages commence with a command such as "say...," that is, God orders a man called "prophet," in a vision or through an angel to say this or that to the people as the Will of God. Thus, their approach is revelatory because God comes to man so that he should love and obey Him; it disqualifies Him as the beloved, the object of search. Therefore, it is only Hinduism which rises as the source of mysticism whereby it is man who seeks God voluntarily.

Yet another reason why mysticism cannot form part of Judaism, Christianity or orthodox Islam is the fact that these religions trust in a creator God, whose relationship with man is that of his Maker. Therefore, man is nothing but God's servant or slave, whose destiny it is to cry, creep and crawl before Him as a worshipper, begging His mercy. Sufis teach to establish a love relationship with God.

Again, the Sematic religion such as Orthodox Islam declares that the ultimate goal of man is to enter paradise to enjoy physical delights while the sect of Islam *i.e.*, Sufism declares that the aim of life is to merge with Ultimate Reality. Similarly, Judaism and Christianity have their ideas of salvation; they treat man as God's creature, dependent on His grace forever. It is only the Upanishadic and Sufistic attitude, 'which seeks union with God or Fana fi Allah.

Before I narrate the basic points of mysticism, which are an integral part of Hinduism, I ought to say a few words about the composition of the Vedas; The Vedas are the treasures of secret knowledge full of spiritual magnitude and poetic beauty. The most pious and excellent among the four in spiritual magnitude is the Ṛig-Veda. Besides the Ṛig-Veda, which is the original work, there are other three volumes known as Yajur, Sāma and Aṭharva.

The Vedas are composed in beautiful classical Sanskrit, it is in Sanskrit that the roots and shoots of such languages as Greek, Latin, Kelt, Tuton and Slovenian lie. Even the deities of these lands their myths, religious beliefs and practices have a good deal in common with the Vedic traditions of thought and action.

This point is so significant that not only comparative religious but also cultural history of the world, and especially the West, cannot be understood without them. Though there is a host of evidence to show that Sanskrit has a precedence over the classical languages of the West, such as Greek and Latin, the western scholars do not acknowledge it as the mother of these tongues, and claim that Sanskrit was a sister of the language they term as the "Indo-European."

Mysticism as depicted in the Ṛig-Veda distinctly shows the following features :

1. Mysticism is not a revealed religion but inspired by the mysterious nature of the universe[9]. This fact is described in hymn CXXXIX of creation :

This hymn clearly states that originally there was neither being nor nonbeing; nor air, nor sky. There was total darkness, and this All was concealed in chaos.

There was only a void and formlessness, and it was the great power of Warmth which led to the birth of unit (*i.e.*, primitive order).

The existent comes out of the non existent, and this is the relationship between being and non being, and was motivated by Desire.

There were mighty forces and their action on "the energy up yonder" which brought order to chaos and gave it form.

One ought to realise that the sage who composed this hymn starts it with speculative questions : what was air and sky covered in? What gave shelter, and was water there and was it unfathomed?

Considering this hymn we can say that it is marvellous to be scientific in all proportions; it clearly states :

a. All was covered in darkness, that is, entire natural phenomenon is of the same origin, hence the principle of monism;
b. the second stunning corollary of the speculative hymn is that existence comes out of nothingness;
c. the third point is that existence is brought about by the action of natural forces on matter *i.e.*, "the energy beyond up yonder,"
d. in the beginning, there was chaos, which was turned into the natural phenomenon that presents order, and
e. behind all this was the great power of warmth, which one may interpret as heat.

However, the kernel of this discussion is that the sage does not pretend that what he says is the revealed message; it is inspired by the wonder and mystery of this universe, and as in the beginning of the hymn, he remains equally astonished in the end :

> "..*Who knows then whence it (the universe) came into being?*

He the first origin of this creation, whether he formed it all or did not form it, whose eye controls this cosmos in the loftiest heaven, he truly knows it, or perhaps he knows not."[10]

2. It is man's instinctive search for the truth, hidden behind the universe, which has been incorporated by Hinduism in its original philosophy. This Indian religion propounds that behind the natural phenomenon, is a principle which is uncreated, eternal, infinite, transcendent and all-embracing. It comprises both being and non-being. This is the sole Reality which is not only the ultimate cause and sources of all existence but also its final goal. This Reality is called Brahman; He is the all, that is, the occult and the visible, over and under; He is not the creator but causes the universe and all that is in it to emanate from Himself.

a. Thus Brahman is in all things and is the self (Atman) of all living things. Brahman, who creates everything out of himself, also is the preserver, transformer and absorber of everything.

b. The fact that the First principle, Brahman or God is in everything and everything comes out of Him, gave birth to the famous Indian philosophy described as the "One in All, and All in One," which the Greeks, the Jews and the Arabs adopted as :

> *"Unity in diversity and diversity in unity." This is monism which is considered as the universal principle of mysticism.*

3. As everything comes out of God and goes back into Him in alternate cycles of evolution and devolution, man's true goal is to seek union with God. This has also become a major doctrine of mysticism.

Communion with God is also an Indian innovation of a later date which emerged with the Bhagavad-Gita, requiring man to love and worship God and seeks nearness of Him. Though this has also become an integral part of mysticism, it is not compatible with the Upanishadic spirit, which happens to be union with God *i.e.*, becoming a part of Him.

4. The hymn XCI of book 10, known as Purusasukta is a further statement of the fact that the world is monistic in nature and emphasizes that the cosmos is not a machine but an organism. If it were not so, man and matter could not form a part of God to make the universe various aspects of the Reality.

Everything on the earth, the sky, the moon, the sun, and even the gods such as Indra, Agni, and Vayu, came into being from the sacrifice of a person called Purusa, having a thousand heads, a thousand eyes and thousand feet.

Delightful though it is to note that this hymn is based on a scientific observation of the universe which diagnoses the oneness of existence, thus enabling man to reach the highest possible point of development, that is, to become a part of God head through union with the Supreme Reality. Though the Hindus have treated Samsara or transmigration of souls from one birth to the next according to the actions done by the individual soul as the vehicle of salvation *i.e.*, the union of man with God, but the oneness of the universe is sufficiently a strong medium to unite man with God.

5. Another major point of the Upanishadic mysticism is the fact that though God is man's superior, the relationship between the two is not that of a master and a slave. The hymn LXXXIX known as Visvadevas clearly states :

"The friendship of the Gods have we devoutly sought."

This Vedic approach is taken much further in verses 3 to 6 of hymn LXXXVIII, dedicated to VARUNA. It says that the worshipper has lost the old favour that he once had of the god, yet he is bold enough to remind the deity :

"What hath become of those our ancient friendship, which without...we walked together?"

The relationship between God and man is that of friendship. Another point this hymn stresses is that man originally belonged to the realm of God, and has been separated from Him. It is this doctrine that appears as the focus of metampsychosis in the systems of Pythagoras, Plato, Gnosticism, and Manichaeism.

6. Meditation through recitation of a particular word which has the mystical power to reform man's inner vision for making his union with God a possibility, is a peculiarity of the Upanishadic mysticism; to the Hindus and Sikhs it is "Japp," which is called Dhikr in Islam; people of other faiths have their own synonyms for this word yet the basic principle is essentially Vedic.

"Simply, ye Mighty Ones, I ask the Gods of that wondrous oblation hallowed by the mystic word." (Hymn CXX–Asvins, Book One).

Again, hymn CLXIV says :

> *"Upon what syllable of holy praise–song, as I were their highest heaven, the Gods repose them, who knows not this, what will he do with praise–song? But they who know it will sit here assembled."*

Originally, "Vasat" was the mystical word in making an oblation to a god with fire. This word had to be used with the utmost accuracy. Otherwise, the priest was sure to suffer the most deadly consequences of his error.

However, the greatest mystical word of the Hindus is OM, which is not only sacred to them but also discloses the nature of mysticism itself. It implies that as God is the self in everything, everything serves as the divine symbol which represents His power, pomp and prestige Of course, a symbol is nothing in itself because its true significance lies in what it represents or stands behind it. It is like a word which has a meaning, it is a flower which has fragrance and it is a magnet which has hidden attractive power. This fact is well illustrated by "OM" itself. It is a Sanskrit word composed of three sounds : a-u-m. The vowels "a" and "u" merge into one another to become o. The mystical approach of Om represents several important articles of the Hindu faith such as the three major Hindu gods. Brahma, Vishnu and

Mahesha, the three Vedic scriptures, Rig. Yajur and Sama, the three worlds of earth, atmosphere and heaven, and so on. In fact, Om represents the mystical essence of the entire universe. This word is frequently used in the Buddhist and Jaina rituals as well as in the practice of yoga and the related techniques of auditory meditation.

The mystical representation by words and syllables is also found in the Koran, the Islamic scripture. It commences with the letters Alif, Lam, Mem which are supposed to have a mystical meaning. "Allah-Hoo" is as significant a word in Islam as Om is in Hinduism. Its frequent recitation or Dhikr is held as the key to salvation, and it is for this reason that it is considered" "Isme-Azam."

This symbolic approach of mysticism is at the root of arts and literature. For example, the written notes are not music but a set of musical cues for the creation of the tones to be produced by the various instruments. Similarly the medium of literature is words but not as abstract entities conceived in the mind but words as spoken or written.

The final stage in the tradition of the Veda is represented by what is called Vedanta *i.e.*, conclusion of the Veda,. This tradition is explained by a vast body of prose and verse rich in speculative elaborations. It is contained in the Upanishads and dates back to 800 B.C. or earlier. This is the fountain of the later Indian philosophy, which itself originated from the Rig-Veda.

Mystical speculation is the special concern of the Upanishads which though gave India a philosophical edge over the rest of mankind, arrested its secular march by creating an observation with the world-to-come and reducing man's role in making this life pleasant, prestigious and praiseworthy. The Hindu concern with the purification of self as a preparation for the other worldliness has imposed a heavy penalty on the Indian way of life.

The Indian wisdom, as it is quite clear from the study of these Upanishads, directed itself with complete devotion, dedication and a sacred sense of duty to the path of Reality; it developed :

a. the concept of a single, Supreme Being, and
b. emphasized that man needs knowledge to discover the Supreme Being and to be able to unite with Him.
c. Though monism had always been the message of the Vedas, through discussion, demonstration and dissemination, the Hindu seers made it a public knowledge that Brahman and self, or God and soul are one in essence. Since everything has a self which is an extension of God, the diversity of forms, constituting this universe, represents a single unity which gave birth to the universal principle: "One in all and all in one."

To a Hindu mystic, Reality is one. The manifoldness of forms is just an appearance :

> *"There is no diversity. He gets death after death, who perceives here seeming diversity. As a unity only is it to be looked upon–*
>
> *This undemonstrable, endurable Being.*[11]*"*

Further in the Upanishads we come across and see that;

> *"The seer sees not death, nor sickness, nor any distress. The seer sees only the All, Obtains the All entirely.*[12]*"*

The Indian philosophy of monism, that is, one in all and all in one, surely holds up the dignity of man. It attaches a negative value to worship or the acts of sacrifice"

> *"This that people say "Worship this god! Worship that god."*
>
> *"And he himself is all the gods"*[13]

So whoever worships another divinity (than his self),

He is one and I another, "is not aware of the truth

> *"An individual man may become Brahma (God) by knowing himself to be such."*[14]

As a matter of interest, I should also mention that Upanishads represent the opposite points of view as well, and thus show the independence and originality of the Indian thinking:

1. To a student of Upanishad, knowledge does not mean "much learning" but the comprehension of the cosmic truth. It is the sole vehicle of discovering the Reality and is directly opposed to the Sematic device of revelation which means that God approaches man to reveal Himself.

In fact, there exist in Upanishads the doctrine or Prasad or Grace, found in Katha 2.20 as well as Svetasvetara 3.20. It means that man needs God's grace to achieve salvation or immortality. Svet 1.6. states :

"In this Brahma–wheel (universe) the soul flutters about, thinking that itself and the Actuator (God) are different, when favoured by Him, it (soul) attains immortality."[15]

Mundaka Upanishad goes even further to negate the doctrine of knowledge and holds out the doctrine of election :

"This soul is not to be obtained by instructions,
not by intellect, nor by much learning.
He is to be obtained only by the One whom He chooses.
To such a one that Soul reveals his own person. "[16]

It is rather stunning that the concepts of Grace and Election which were to form the basic doctrines of Christianity and Islam centuries later were developed in India as part of the mystical system.

Having said that I should emphasize that the doctrine of knowledge remains the true mystical Vedic approach. Though I have already propounded it in my own way, I may now explain it as Shankra, the celebrated Indian philosopher did, centuries earlier:

The concept of Maya is to be found in the Rig-Veda 6.47.18, where it means "supernatural powers or artifices" which imply the antithesis of Reality; this is the origin of the Vedic doctrine of Maya : it means that the real Brahma or God is the undifferenced unity but the natural phenomena which appear as self subsistent entities, are unreal and result from a person's own ignorance or Avidya which projects the things or one's own sense as the ultimate being of the world.

However, this ignorance can be remedied through knowledge. This is what gave birth to the celebrated Indian theory of cosmic illusion which served as the basis of the plantonic theory of Forms and an essential pillar of the mysticism. This fact is described in the following verse of the Upanishad.

"This whole world the illusion maker projects out of this (Brahma). And in it by illusion the other is confined.
Now one should know that Nature is illusion.
And that the Mighty Lord is the illusion maker[17]."

Shankra stated the theory of Maya much more forcefully. He held the world does not exist of itself but is derived from Brahman (God) and depends on Him for its existence. Therefore, it is not an illusion but less real. It is a Maya, a phenomenal appearance, partly created by our own imagination; it expresses our inability to see the world without being an expression of cause and change. It shows man's innate limitation which is termed as Avidya or ignorance. Because of this Maya, the intellect assumes that it knows the real. The world is only one Being but through Maya (Avidya) appears as multiplicity of forms and a process of flux. Change is just a name for superficial fluctuation of forms. Behind this Maya, forms and vicissitudes, lies the Reality that can be reached not by sensation but through insight gained by knowledge. This ultimate Reality is Brahman (God).

Since God is in all, the Self or Atman (soul) or everything is a part of God. It is shared by us and everything else; the undivided Self or things, which happens to be omnipresent, is identical with Brahman, who is neuter and above all human attributes, desire and ends.

Shankra, a great mystic, set the goal of mysticism. He believed that destination of philosophy is to discover the secret behind the universe, and the ultimate goal of every seeker is to lose himself into this secret. This is what Muslims call "Fana-Fe-Allah" and other remembers it as Union with God. This is the stage of existence where there is no misery, no death. It is a state of Ananda, the blissful peace but it cannot be achieved unless a man not only renounces the world but also himself.

It is basically the Indian Mysticism which has been practiced in various forms throughout the world. Mysticism is the product of India though this fact has not been acknowledged fully owing to ignorance and bigotry. The above mentioned forms of mysticism are likely to establish their origin and demonstrate that being a search for the hidden truth, mysticism is man's true religion. It is the mystery in which resides the delight of mankind. The whole philosophy of almost all Upanishads is centered round the concept of the Self and this Self is no other than the Brahman. This Brahman is bodyless, deathless beyond time and place is beyond sense perception and is unknowable yet the Upanishads stated that this Self or the Brahman can be realized by concentration or by Dhikra or contemplation. The divine word AUM is the symbol of this Supreme Self and by focusing on the divine syllable and by contemplating on AUM one can realize the self and thereby realize the Brahman. In the chapters that follow we shall see what the nature of this supreme Reality is and how one can realize the Self. Let us now proceed to decipher the mystery of the Vendanta in the chapters to follow and at the same time deciphering the hidden Reality of the Tasawwuf or the Islamic Mysticism.

References

1. ﷺ means Sallaloho Alayhi-wasllam Peace Be Upon Him in short PBUH. This is a respectful utterance and used only after the name of the Prophet Mohammed. I have used this Arabic symbol at all places where the Prophet' name is used.
2. Exodus, 3:4.
3. Matthew, 10:37.
4. Luke 14:26.
5. Sahih Muslim Vol. 1-I Mohsin Khan.
6. Suhagiya Sect of Sufism.
7. See glossary at the end.
8. Seers gone mad in the path to realize the Supreme Reality.
9. This fact is described in hymn CXXXIX of creation.
10. *Ibid.,* p. 17.
11. Brihadaranyaka Upanishad, 4.4.19-20.
12. Chandogya Upanishad, 7.26.2.

13. Brihadaranyaka Upanishad, 1.4.6.
14. *Ibid.,* 1.4.15.
15. Katha Upanishad, 2.23.
16. Mundaka Upanishad, 3.2.3.
17. Svet. Upanishads, 4.9-10.

Chapter 2

Major Upanishads and Mysticism in Them

Upanishads are the sacred texts of Hinduism; they are universal in their subject matter and touch each of the human beings. They are the concluding portion of the Vedas therefore they are called in a group as 'Vendanta'–the end or culmination of the Vedas, since they are considered the last of the 'Sruti,' the revealed wisdom of the Rishis. The Rishis have seen directly into the heart of Reality; in that sense the wisdom of the Vedas is considered timeless and authorless. Later teachers evolved the tradition by interpreting and expanding upon the central philosophy; these commentaries are known as 'smriti' and, while not considered to be revelatory, have nonetheless had considerable impact on Indian thought.

Dr. Yajneshvar Shastri says, "The Upanishads shift the centre of interest from Vedic gods to the Reality behind changing phenomena. Upanishadic seers turned the vision more inward and gave a new direction to spiritual life. That permanent eternal and unchanging Reality is called the Brahman or the Atman, which is existence, consciousness and Bliss."

Upanishadic literature also concentrates on Self–the inner controller of human being. It analyses the Self and distinguishes between its outer layer and inner Reality. The real self is pure consciousness. Not being limited by anything; it is infinite. The real Self is called Atman. Everyone contains Divinity within him and there is no difference between the individual self and the Ultimate Self or the Ultimate Reality-the Brahman. Katha Upanishad reveals the truth by stating that, this self is concealed in all things and does not appear to but is perceived by the keen insight aided by sharp and penetrating intellect.

Regarding the mystical aspect of the Upanishads we can say that *Upanishad* means the inner or mystical teaching. The term Upanishad is derived from *upa* (near), *ni* (down) and *s* (*h*) *ad* (to sit), *i.e.*, sitting down near. Groups of acolytes sit near the master to learn from him the secret doctrine. In the quietness of the forest hermitages, the Upanishadic thinkers pondered on the problems of deepest concerns and communicated their knowledge to fit pupils near them. Shankara derives the word Upanishad as a substitute from the root sad, 'to loosen,' 'to reach' or 'to destroy' with UPa and ni as prefixes. If this interpretation is accepted, Upanishad means The knowledge of the Brahman after the removal of the veil of ignorance. In this sense those treatises that deal with Brahman-knowledge are called the Upanishads. The different derivations together make out that the Upanishads give us both divine vision and arguments seeking the Truth. There is a core of certainty that is in essence inexpressible except by a way of life. It is by a rigorous meditation and contemplation on the Self that one can reach the Reality.

The Upanishads more clearly put forward the prime vedic canon like Self-realization, yoga and meditation, karma and reincarnation, which were hidden or kept veiled under the symbols of the older obscure religion. The Upanishads are usually linked with a particular veda, through a Brahmana or Aranyaka.

The subject matter of almost all the Upanishads is the Self which is Brahman itself. The Self and how to realize Self is the focal point in all the Upanishads. Self or Atman or Brahman is at the centre of all the Upanishads and everything else rotates round the Self.

The main figure in the Upanishads, though not present in many of them, is the sage Yajnavalkya. Most of the great teachings of later Hindu and Buddhist philosophy derive from him. He taught the great doctrine of "neti-neti", the view that truth can be found only through the negation of all thoughts about it. Other important Upanishadic sages are Uddalaka Aruni, Shwetaketu, Shandilya, Aitareya, Pippalada, and Sanat kumara. many earlier Vedic teachers like Manu, Brihaspati, Ayasya and Narada are also found in the Upanishads.

The spiritual meanings of the Vedic texts are brought out and emphasized in their own right in the Upanishads.

The earlier Vedas are concerned with Vedic religious rituals and the importance of sacrifice. The Upanishads herald the beginning of the profound stream of Indian exploratory thought. Composed probably by various, mostly unknown, seers, these teachings are less philosophical and more mystical in nature, and contain the fundamental core of Indian metaphysics. They are varied but deeper common threads can be discerned. The word 'Upanishad' also means 'secret teaching;' this reflects the longstanding oral tradition in India, where this knowledge was passed down from teacher to disciple directly. Some would also say that it refers to the mystical nature of the Upanishadic revelations themselves that is this divine knowledge was passed traditionally from Guru to Shishya. It is not sufficient merely to grasp the ideas intellectually; a true realization requires an immediate experience of a transcendent Reality which one cannot put into words, and which is the focus of the upanishadic teachings. Regarding the intuitive, mystical nature of the Upanishads, it should be noted that the basis of the philosophy is highly practical; that is, it is not concerned with mere speculation, but only with addressing those issues that relate directly to the conditions of life and their improvement. Keeping this view in their mind the western philosophers take Upanishads as mere speculation and distort the mystical and hidden Reality in Upanishads. The Rishis knew that in order to improve life, one must ask basic questions concerning the basic nature of Reality and of human beings, and the ultimate goal of human existence. This speculative exploration marked the beginning of the Upanishads. Now let us analyse how different major Upanishads have interwoven in themselves these mystical aspect of the supreme Reality.

The Mandukya Upanishad

Mandukya Upanishad belongs to the Atharva Veda. It contains twelve mantras. Bridging the gap between the spontaneous and ecstatic mysticism of the early Upanishads and the systematic metaphysics of Advaitic Vedanta this short but influential Upanishad, refers to four states of consciousness. The are as under :

1. waking or gross,
2. dreaming or subtle,
3. dreamless sleep or very subtle, and
4. the Absolute or Self (Atman).

These aspects are related to each other with the three letters of the important Vedic mantra AUM, with the fourth principle indicating silence (the Unmanifest). The Mandukya Upanishads reveals the mystery of the word AUM and stresses to meditate upon this beautiful and mystical three letter syllable. The world is a mystery and the Supreme Reality is also a mystery hidden into the three letter word Aum. The seer can realize the Brahman or the Ultimate Reality by concentrating on this pious word. Everything is included or hidden in AUM. The past, present and the future is Aum. AUM is beyond time and space beyond Spatio-temporality yet encompasses everything animate and inanimate into its sphere. It is said that this Upanishad is enough to lead one to liberation.

Mandukyam ekam evalam mumuksunam vimuktaye

This is the mystery of the Supreme Reality and is hidden into this Supreme word AUM.

Now let us see the relevant Mantras of this short Upanishad:

sarvam hy etad Brahman, ayam atman Brahman, so'yam atma catus-pati[1]

(...this self (Atman)is Brahman. This same self has four quarters.)

jagrita sthano bahis prajnaha saptanga
ekonavimsati-mukhah
sthul-bhug vaisvanarah prathamah padah[2]

[The first quarter is *vaishvanara*, whose sphere is the waking state (jagarat, the world), who cognises (*prajna*) external objects...]

The second quarter is taijasa, whose sphere is the dream (*svapna*) state, who cognises (*prajna*) internal objects...

...The third quarter is prajna, whose sphere is deep sleep (*sushupta*), who has become one, who is verily a mass of cognition (*prajna*), who is full of bliss and who enjoys bliss whose face is thought.

This is the lord of all, this is the knower of all, this is the inner controller; this is the source of all; this is the beginning and end of beings.

(*Turiya*) is not that which cognises the inner, not that which cognises the outer, not that which cognises both of them, not a mass of cognition, not cognitive, not non-cognitive. Unseen, incapable of being spoken of, upgraspable, without any distinctive marks, unthinkable, unnameable, the essence of the knowledge of the one self, that into which the world is resolved, the peaceful, the benign, the non-dual, such, they think is the fourth (*turiya*) quarter. He is the self (*Atman*); He is to be known.

In this Upanishad, the four quarters are four aspects of the one Reality : the four-fold classification of existence into the objective, subjective, consciousness, and transcendent-Absolute, states of consciousness. Therefore, Turiya is the Transcendent Absolute Reality, the Atman. Prajna here refers to the cosmic dimension of bliss or consciousness, which is identified with the Supreme Reality. The other two quarters, Taijasa and Vishva or Vaishvanara, represent the inner and outer, subtle and gross, psychic and physical, dimensions of the Individual being. The word Taijasa actually means "bright" or "shining".

It is not the highest but the second highest principle, Prajna or consciousness, which is identified as the source of all; the beginning and end of beings. This is actually an emanationist idea; in that Emanationism assumes the First Principle or Absolute to be too transcendent to be actually involved in Creation. It is also in keeping with the Indian Vedantic tradition, which sees the cosmic goodhead as inferior to the Absolute : inasmuch as one accesses the Absolute in the essence of one's own being (the Atman), one transcend even the Gods, for one become one's self as well. Thus, the Vedantic monist Shankara sees the Jiva or individual soul, the Brahman, as both equally non-absolute manifestations of the one Reality.

These four states of consciousness of the Upanishads can well be compared with the four states of Sufism or Islamic mysticism. They are : (1) The Shari's (2) The Tariqa (3) The Marifa and (4) The Haqiqa. These four stages of Islamic mysticism corresponds to the four states as propounded by the Upanishads. When one crosses the boundary of Vaishvanara one enters the second reign of consciousness that is taijas. In this state one tries to divert the senses inwardly and remains detached from the outward senses. The soul becomes the guiding light. The Tariqua of Islamic mysticism also stresses on contemplation of Allah the Supreme Reality. Many Sufis called this state as inward journey. The third state of consciousness prajna of the Upanishads can well be compared with the Marifa of Sufism and the fourth turiya with The Haqiqa of Islamic Mysticism. In the Haqiqa, one merges with Allah the Supreme Reality. It is also known as Fana. When one realizes the Self and merges with the Supreme Reality, ANAL-HAQ or AHAMBRAH-MASMI spontaneously flows out from one's inner being like water from the torrent. This state is the state of Fana or the supreme state of realisation of the self or merging of the soul with the Supreme soul. In the words of Shankara one sees SARVAM KHALU IDAM BRAHMAN and one realizes BRAHMAN STYAM JAGAT MITHYA JIVOH BRAHMAH EVA NAPARAH, and the Sufi mystics like Hallaj Mansur, Sarmad and Hamdani spontaneously utter ANAL HAQ. It comes automatically without any strain or stress. When it happens it happens abruptly and instantly like a thunder bolt. But it happens only to the seers or to the Sufi mystics. It happens only to Astavakra or Janaka, or Shankara or Mansur or Sarmad.

Kena Upanishad : The *Kena Upanishad* derives its name from the first word Kena, by whom, and belongs to the Sama Veda. It is also known as the *Talavakara,* the name of the *Brahmana* of the *Sama Veda* to which the Upanishad belongs.

It has four segments, two in verse and two in prose. The melodious segment deals with the Supreme Brahman, the supreme principle underlying the world of phenomenon and the prose part of the Upanishad deals with the Supreme as God, Isvara. The knowledge of the Absolute, para vidya, which secures immediate liberation (sadyo-mukti) is possible only for those who are able to pull out their thoughts and senses from material objects and focus on the ultimate fact of the universe. The knowledge of Isvara, apara vidya, puts one on the pathway that leads to liberation ultimately which is called karma-mukti. The worshipping soul slowly but surely attains the superior wisdom that results in the consciousness of the identity with the Supreme Reality.

Commenting upon verse 4 of the kena Upanishad Swami Krishnanand in Essays on the Upanishads says that :

"Consciousness should be realised as the fundamental basis of all mental experiences. It should be realised in every state of our life in waking, dreaming and deep sleep. All thoughts are heterogeneous in their nature. They are not connected with one another. But they are experienced as belonging to one person because of the unity of the Self within. Our body, senses and mind are all made up of scattered parts that appear to be a unified whole because of the underlying indivisible essence. If only the Self were not there, our personality would be thrown away into the condition of atoms, disconnected and varied. There is no difference at all between the building bricks of one body and of another body. All are made up of the same earth, water, fire, air and space. But bodies appear to be different, they act in different ways, because the actor is not the body. Differences are in the desires within. This shows that man is not the body. When we speak to a person we do not speak to the body at all; we speak to the character hidden within. Even the ultimate constituents of this inner character do not differ from person to person. The same force acts as the substantial essence of all kinds. But this substances of minds whirls in different directions at different centres of existence, thus creating differences. This whirling is called the mind, and this way of whirling is called a desire. Therefore, desires differ from person to person, and consequently bodies also appear to be different, as the body is controlled by the mind. With all these distracting characteristics which a person is made up of, he appears to be a whole being, without differences at all. The external ugliness is hidden by the reflection of the inner beauty of the Self. This synthesising nature belongs to consciousness and not to thought. The states of waking, dreaming and deep sleep differ from one another, and yet, a person feels that he alone exists during these three states, without difference. He identifies himself as a single unity in all changes that take place, whether in mind or in body. Waking, dreaming and deep sleep are mental conditions, manifested, slightly manifested and unmanifested. But the Self is neither the manifest nor the unmanifest. It is immutable. It is the General Ground underlying all particulars. Particulars are deviations from the natural Truth. All particularities are self imposed, *i.e.*, created by the individuals. But the generality of the essence is common to all. Even the particulars have no life and value without this general being, even as a pot has no value without clay."

Samyagdarshana is correct perception of things as they really are. It is a spiritual condition and not an act. It has no concern with the changes that take place in the body and even in the surface consciousness of the mind. It is, in other words, simple knowing. All objectives knowledge breeds birth and death, because knowledge of objects means an underlying desire for objects. We cannot think of anything without having a love for it, positive or negative, and every love is a deviation from the law of Self Existence. When we love an object, we deny ourselves, or rather, we deceive ourselves, because we, thereby, sell ourselves to that object. Because the object changes itself, and because our love for that object also hunts, after it, and because our love is inseparable from ourselves, we appear to die when the object vanishes, and take rebirth in order to find that object of love. Perception of diversity means moving from death to death, because we are courting thereby self transformation, due to our desire for identifying ourselves with the diverse forms of objects.

Self-knowledge, therefore, consists in self identical, immediate, non-relational knowledge. Knowledge, however, cannot be an attribute of the Self. If so, what is the nature of the Self? We cannot say that the Self is other than consciousness, holding that consciousness is its attribute. Else, the Self would be unconciousness, which, however, is not our experience. The Self is not a substance having attributes. If consciousness is an attribute of the Self, there would be rise and fall of the knowledge of the Self. It is not possible for us to say what would be the nature of the Self in essence, if it is not consciousness. Without consciousness, it would become a dull substance, ever changing, partitioned, impermanent and impure, which conclusion is, however, illogical.

The theory that the knowledge of the Self is the result of the contact of the Self with the mind is incorrect. This theory reduces the Self to unconsciousness. Several of the declarations of the Srutis (Upanishads) would be contradicted by this theory. Because the Self is all pervading, there would be an eternal contact of the Self with the mind, as wherever the mind is, the Self also is. What, then, is the meaning of remembrance and forgetfulness? There would be no forgetfulness at all because of the perpetual contact of the Self with the mind. Moreover, it is wrong to hold that the Self can be in contact with anything, because the Upanishads deny such a possibility. Only a substance with attributes can be in contact with another substance with attributes. The mind has attributes, but the Self has none. Infinity cannot be in contact with perishability. The knowledge of the Self is not the effect of its contact with the mind, as the acceptance of this theory would be to accept that consciousness itself is transient. The Self is eternal knowledge in its very essence. It does not require any contact.

There is another theory which holds that the Self knows itself by itself, by becoming the subject as well as the object. This theory makes the Self perishable, because it divides the Self into two parts. The Self can never become an object of itself. If it does, it has to die. One thing cannot become another thing unless it dies to that one thing. The Self does not require another consciousness to know itself. Therefore it cannot be said that the Self becomes an object to know itself.

Ishopanishad : The main theme of this Upanishad is Path of knowledge versus path of action and the Self (Atman) and how to realize the Self. The benedictory or prayer mantra establishes the supremacy and completeness of Brahman in the following verse :

Om puranam adah purnam idam purnat purnam udachyte,
Purnasya purnamadaya purnam evavashishyate.
Om shantih, shantih, shantih.

[All this is full. All that is full.
From fullness, fullness comes.
When fullness is taken from fullness,
Fullness still remains.
O M shanti shanti shanti]

This mantra describes the fullness of the Brahman. If from fullness taken out fullness still fullness remains this is the mystery of the Brahman. This mantra brings out the mystery of the universe through the cause and effect relationship. **Purnam adah purnam idam**, meaning : *"That is complete, this is complete."* The word adah (That) refers to the Supreme Atma, Paramatma (the cause) and the word idam (this) refers to the entire animate and inanimate manifestation (the effect) pervaded by the Supreme Atma or the Ultimate Reality. The Supreme Atma is beyond this manifestation and is indescribably greater. Further, purnat purnam udacyate, meaning : "From the complete (Paramatma), only the complete manifestation (this universe) has emanated, because incomplete cannot be the result of the complete. The doctrine is:

"Whatever is there in the causal form, that itself changes into the effect form. The effect of the complete cannot be incomplete." Further, the mantra declares : Purnasya purnam adaya purnam eva avashishyate. Meaning : "From That complete when this complete is negated, is taken away, what remains is still complete." It might look absurd, but it can be understood by way of an example. When taking away zero from zero, the result is still zero. Similarly subtracting infinity from infinity, what remains is still infinity. If zero is put before anything as prefix the value decreases and it put as suffix the value increases, likewise the manifest world with Brahman multiplies into millions and billions folds but when one realizes the Self one becomes merged with this Supreme Zero that is the Ultimate Reality.

In this mantra, it has been declared that every living being is complete in itself as the Supreme Atma is. There may be difference in size and form, but in essence and quality there is no difference. The Shruti (Veda) also says Ayamatma Brahma, Sohamasmi–This Atma is Brahma, I am that. Once it is realized that the Atma manifested in our form is complete Sat-Cid-Ananda, self-consciousness increases greatly. If there is still any doubt about our own totality despite the declaration of the Vedas, then, inquire why is there such a feeling? But for this, one has to take recourse in Brahmavidya; surrender to a self realized master of this knowledge. After the benedictory mantra, the Ishopanishad gives an unparalleled message to the mankind. This message is for the uplift of mankind and for the seers this message lead them to realize the Supreme Reality and the Sufis imbibe this message into their soul and become one with the Almighty God by Tariqat, Marifat and become absorbed (Fana-Fi-Allah).

The Aitareya Upanishad

The Aitareya Upanishad is one of the oldest of the Upanishads. It belongs to the Aitareeya Aranyaka of the Rigveda. It is divided into three chapters and contains 33 verses. The Upanishad deals with the process of creation.

The first chapter discusses the creation of Purusha, (the primal Being in its macrocosmic form and man in its microcosmic facet), the creation of the various divinities, and how they were placed and assigned various duties. Section three of the first chapter narrates how food was created and how various divinities sought to control it, but failed. In the last few verses of this section we are explained how the self entered the body and stayed there as the enjoyer.

The second chapter is more difficult to understand. We are explained here the three births of the self.

The third chapter deals with the qualities of the Self or Brahman. It contains one of the most famous expressions of the Vedanta, "prajnanam Brahma," which means Brahman is intelligence.

This Upanishad is written in symbolic language and therefore it is necessary to decipher its mystery in its true spirit. It is full of mystery. The creation of the world is very magnificently depicted in the following verse.

From Brahman came space; from space, air from air, fire from fire, water from water, Earth from Earth, plants from plants; food; and from food the human body, head, arms, legs, and heart.[3]

Further the same Upanishad depicts in the form of a prayer a desire of the soul to merge with the Ultimate Reality.

O Lord of love, revealed in the scriptures, who have assumed the forms of all creatures, grant me wisdom to choose the path that can lead me to immorality.[4]

O Lord of love, may I enter into you, and may you reveal yourself unto me, the[5] *pure one masquerading as many. You are the refuge of all devotees. I am your devotee. Make me your own.*

Katha Upanishad

The Katha Upanishad reveals before us the mystery of life and earth and drive home the idea that the self is deathless and indestructible and unaffected by the spatio-temporarality. The following is the prayer Mantra and what follows is the story of Nachiketa with the God of Death Yama. The story is significant to discuss in detail because it has in it the very core of mysticism.

> *"May He protect us both together by revealing knowledge. May He protect us both by vouchsafing the results of knowledge. May we attain vitality together. Let what we study be stimulating. May we not complain at each other."*

Upanishads are based on the dialogue between a realized Soul acting as the Teacher, Rishi, and a sincere seeker of Truth who approaches Him as a disciple. In Katha Upanishad the instructor is Yama–The Death Himself–and the learner is a young Nachiketa in his youth. This Upanishad is one of the most popular Upanishads for its simplicity[7] and clarity in making the subject matter regarding the Ultimate Reality comprehensible very easily. It contains 120 verses. This Upanishad as I have said above is the Upanishad discussing the subject of the eternality of the Soul. The self is nothing but the Brahman itself and hence Nachiketa enters into dialogue with the Yama. Let us see the story itself that will reveal before us like the tapestry of events as if we are seeing them before our eyes.

The story runs as under :

Vajashrava, Nachiketa's father, decided to acquire fruits of sacrificial rites performed Viswajit yajna in which the performer had to give away all his valuable belongings. Cows were considered valuable and special possessions in those days, and hence Vajashrava decided to donate all his cows to Brahmins.

Nachiketa was in his youth, and he was observing the sacrificial ritual with innocent interest. However, he was surprised to notice that his father was giving away only old and feeble cows, cows 'which had given up yielding milk and were not capable of breading calves'.

This 'shrewdness' of his father ignited profound change in Nachiketa's heart. Nachiketa, in order to dissuade his father from engaging in further means acts, asked, "O father, to whom have you decided to give me away?" Initially, the father did not take any notice of this 'childish' question, but Nachiketa was insistent. He repeated the question thrice when the irritated father said, "All right, O Nachiketa, I give you to Death."

Thus ordained, young Nachiketa went to the kingdom of Yama–The Death–where he waited for the return of Death from his duties. On his return, Yama was told about the 'Brahmin boy waiting for him for there days without food or water'.

Yama praised sincerity of Nachiketa to wait for him, but as he was responsible for keeping a Brahmin boy waiting for him granted three boons to Nachiketa for three days waiting.

The Boons : The three boons sought by Nachiketa and granted by Yama are as under:

The First Boon

"O Death, of the three boons you have offered me, I ask for the first to the effect that my father may become free from worry about me and take me and talk to me when freed by you. "The boon was granted.

The Second Boon

As the second boon Nachiketa asked for granting him the knowledge of the means to attain higher life in the heaven and immortality.

There is a dialogue between Yama and the boy about the primordial Fire and sacrificial rituals to attain to heavenly life Yama tells him about the methods and ways of performing these yajnas etc. Death tells him that only the enlightened one becomes fit to go to heaven. In heaven there is no fear, fear of old age, etc. having transcended both hunger and thirst, and crossed over grief, one enjoys in the heavenly world.

The Third Boon

Then comes the main subject matter of this Upanishad. As regards his third boon, Nachiketa wants to know :

"This doubt that arises, consequent on the death of a man–some saying 'it) (The SELF) exists', and others saying 'It (The SELF) does not exist'. I would like to know this, under your instruction, O Death, what is the Truth". 1.i.20

Nachiketa had asked for the ultimate knowledge. What is death, what is after death! What is Reality and what is Truth. Yama tries to dissuade the young boy from going into these subtle questions of immense intricacies for Death was not sure whether Nachiketa was qualified to receive this knowledge for which only an occasional and rare aspires.

Yama exhorts Nachiketa to ask for health, life, riches, jewels, and enjoyment. 'Ask for lasting kingdom and armies, ask for anything in this world or of heaven, I will grant you all this as your third boon, but do not force me to go into the secrets of life and death. Do not insist for ultimate knowledge.'

"Ask for sons and grandsons that will be hundreds of years old. Ask for many animals, elephants and gold, and horses, and vast spread of the earth. And you yourself live for as many years as you like." 1.i.23. "If you think some other boon to be equal to this, ask for that. Ask for wealth and long life. O nachiketa, you become a ruler over a vast region. I make you fit for the enjoyment of all delicious things." 1.i.24.

"Whatever things there be that are desirable but difficult to get–pray for all those cherished things according to your choice. Here are these women with chariots and musical instruments–such are surely not to be had by mortals. With these, who are offered by me, you get yourself served. O Nachiketa do not inquire about death." 1.i.25.

But Nachiketa argues that all worldly treasures and heavenly pleasures come to an end sooner or later. If not day after, after hundred years. These are not permanent means of enjoyment. Nachiketa says, "O Death, transient are these, and they waste away the vigour of all the organs that a man has. All life without exception is short indeed. Let the vehicles be yours alone; let the dances and songs be yours." 1.i.26.

He insists to get the ultimate knowledge of Self, 'for, O Death, you have promised me the third boon'. Seeing the determination, faith, sincerity, and perseverance of Nachiketa, seeing him to be the perfect disciple, Death agrees to tell him about the Ultimate Reality : Brahman or Atman.

Death says, "The preferable is different indeed; and so, indeed, is the pleasurable different. These two, serving divergent purposes, bind men. Good befalls him who accepts the preferable among these two. He who selects pleasurable over preferable falls from the true end." 1.ii.1.

"The preferable and pleasurable approach man. The man of intelligence, having considered them, separates the two. The intelligent one selects the delectable for the sake of growth and protection of the body, etc." 1.ii.2

"O Nachiketa, you, such as you are, have discarded, after consideration all the desirable things that are themselves delightful or are the producers of delight. You have not accepted this path of wealth in which many a man comes to grief." 1.ii.3

"Living in the midst of ignorance and considering themselves intelligent and enlightened, the senseless people go round and round following crooked ways just like the blind led by the blind." 1.ii.5

"This wisdom that you have, O Nachiketa, which leads to sound knowledge when imparted only someone else, other than logician, by the wonderful expounder, is not to be attained through argumentation. You are, O compassionate one, ingrained with true resolution. May our question be like you, O Nachiketa!" 1.ii.9

And as Death goes on elaborating the subtlety and nuances of means and methods to achieve that transcendental state, consciousness of Nachiketa also is getting established in that altered state to experience the Truth.

"The intelligent man gives up happiness and sorrow by developing concentration of mind on the SELF and thereby meditating on the old Deity who is inscrutable, lodged inaccessibly, located in the intellect, and seated in the midst of misery." 1.ii.12.

"The SELF is neither born nor does it die. It did not originate from anything, nor did anything originate from it. It is birthless, eternal, undecaying, and primordial. It is not injured even when it is killed." 1.ii.18. "The SELF that is subtler than the subtle, and greater than the great, is lodged in the heart of every creature. A desireless man sees the glory of the SELF through the serenity of the organs and thereby he becomes free from sorrow." 1.ii.20. And on and on goes the dialogue between the two great knowers of the Truth..

It is wonderful fact that if the Teacher and the taught are of highest qualifications, it is a matter of minutes to enter the state of Samadhi. As the Teacher explains so does the disciple experiences the Truth spoken. Nachiketa gets established into highest state of bliss where knowledge of Brahman becomes a fact of direct experience'. The same thing can be seen when Arjuna experiences the cosmic form of Sri Krishna when the Lord is telling him the Gita!"

The Upanishads are the treasurers of the Spiritual knowledge. They are the torrents flowing with nectar that any one can drink the manna from them and make his/her life meaningful. The seers of the Upanishads have left for us the Divine chest full of spiritual knowledge and at the same time they have also left the key to this Divine knowledge not anywhere else but they have left the key with us only. The key is meditation and austerities and we can find this key which is hidden in our heart by meditation on the Supreme Reality. This Supreme Reality is the Self or the Brahman or the consciousness. But this Brahman consciousness must not be mixed up with ordinary consciousness. The ordinary consciousness because of Māya or Avidya becomes the hurdle in the path of meditation and thereby Self realization. Regarding the ordinary consciousness Swami Krishnananda says :

"The definition of Brahman as consciousness should not be mistaken to be an attempt to bring down the nature of Brahman to the level of our understanding. We say Brahmaṇ is consciousness because nothing of this world is conscious. It is just to differentiate reality from appearance that we term Brahman consciousness. It is to exalt it and not lower it. Even when we accept that Brahman is Sat or Chit we do not confuse it with anything that we know. It is beyond the Sat and the Chit which we know. We reject everything which we know and refuse to be satisfied with anything that comes to us as an experience. We may have the highest possession of experience, but we have to abandon it. Whatever experience one may have, grand and glorious, one should not be under the impression that one's achievement is over. It is an infinite rejection of things and states that we have to practise. There is no end for our denials. One cannot suspect whether one is in the state of Brahman or in a state to be denied. It will be clear when one experiences it. Dissatisfaction and the awareness of 'I'-ness will be the indicators of the imperfection of a particular state of experience. Brahman is doubtless existence and we can experience Brahman only after self effacement. It is not easy to know it." The subject matter of almost all the Upanishads is the Self or the Brahman. They do differ in style and versification but the content remains the same through all the major Upanishads and it is only the Self or the Brahman. The Brihadaranyak talks about the deathlessness of the soul. Kena talks about the cause behind every living and non living being, and Taittiriya and Aitariya talk about the manifestations of the Brahman. The Ishopanishad is beyond comparison. It is par excellence in Brahman knowledge. Extolling the beauty and content of the Isha upanishad Mahatma Gandhi has said; "If all the Upanishads and all the scriptures happened all of a sudden to be reduced to ashes, and if only the first verse of the Ishopanishad were left in the memories of the Hindus, Hinduism would live forever." This is the beauty of the Upanishads and this is the magnanimity of their ambience, and vastness of their spiritual depth. Upanishads are not merely the scattered utterances of the Rishis, they are complete in all respect and the tying thread that binds them all with the Self which occupies the pivotal position in pages of the Upanishads. The central theme running throughout almost all the Unpanishad is the discussion of the Self and realization of it through contemplation.

Chapter 3

Tasawwuf (Sufism) or Islamic Mysticism

The word Tasawwuf is Arabic word which means Islamic mysticism. The western scholars prefer to translate the word Tasawwuf as Sufism. Hujwiri says, "Sufi is a name which is given and has formerly been given to the perfect saint and spiritual adepts. One of the Shayikh says : *"Man saffahu 'i-hubb fa-huwa saf wa man safafahu 'I-habib fa-huwa sufiyy." "He that is purified by love is pure, and he that is absorbed in the Beloved and has abandoned all else is a Sufi."*

Tasawwuf or Sufism (the translation usually preferred in the West) is the name of the ways Sufis follow to reach God, the Truth. While the term *Tasawwuf* usually expresses the theoretical or philosophical aspect of the search for truth, its practical aspect is usually referred to as 'being a dervish.'

Tasawwuf has been defined in many ways. According to some, *Tasawwuf* is Almighty God's annihilating man with respect to his ego and self-centeredness and then reviving him spiritually with the lights of His Essence; in other words, God's annihilating man with respect to his own will and then directing him by His Own Will. Another approach to Tasawwuf sees it as the continuous striving to get rid of all kinds of bad maxims and evil conduct and acquiring virtues.

Junayd-al-Baghdadi, a famous Sufi master, defines Tasawwuf as a way by which to recollect 'self annihilation in God" and 'permanence or subsistence with God.' Shibli's definition is summarized as being always together with God or in His ever presence while aiming at nothing wordly or even other-wordly. Abu Muhammad Jariri describes it as resisting the temptations of the carnal self and bad moral qualities and acquiring laudable moral qualities.

There are some who describe Tasawwuf as seeing behind the [outward] Reality of things and events and interpreting whatever happens [in the world] in relation with God Almighty. Then, by regarding every act of the Almighty as a window to 'see' Him, living one's life in continuous effort to view or 'see' Him with a profound, spiritual 'seeing' indescribable in physical terms, and living in profound awareness of being continually overseen by Him.

All the accounts just given can be summed up as follows :

Tasawwuf means that by being freed from the vices and weaknesses particular to human nature and acquiring angelic qualities and conduct pleasing to God, one lives one's life in accordance with the requirements of knowledge and love of God and in the spiritual delight that comes thereby.

Tasawwuf is based on observing the rules of Shari'a down to good manners and penetrating their (inward) meaning. An initiate or traveller upon the path (salik) who can succeed in this never separates the outward observance of Shari'a from its inward dimension and carries out all the requirements of both the outward and inward dimensions of religion. Through such observance, he travels toward the goal in utmost humility and submission.

Tasawwuf is a path leading to knowledge of God and is a way demanding solemnity [of bearing and purpose]. There is no room in it for negligent or frivolous manners. It requires that the initiate should be like a honeybee flying from the hive to flowers and from flowers to the hive, continuously striving in pursuit of knowledge of God. He should purify his heart from all attachments other than seeking God, and resist all inclinations and desires and appetites of his carnal self. He should also lead his life at a spiritual level with a readiness to receive Divine blessings and inspirations and in strict observance of the Prophetic example. Sincerely admitting attachment and adherence to God as the greatest merit and honour, he should renounce his own desires for the sake of the demands of God, the Truth or the ultimate Reality.

After these [preliminary] definitions, we should discuss the aim, benefits and principles of Tasawwuf :

Tasawwuf requires strict observance of the religious obligations and austerity in life-style, the renunciation of animal or worldly apetites.

Tasawwuf aims, by purifying man's heart and employing his senses and faculties in the way of God, to live a life at the spiritual level. Tasawwuf also enables man, through constant performance of the acts of worshipping God, to deepen his consciousness of being a servant of God or at a highest level the lover of God. It enables him to renounce the world with respect to its transient dimension and the face of it that is turned to human desires and fancies, and awakens him to the other world and to the face of this world that is turned toward the Divine Beautiful Names.

The benefit of Tasawwuf is that man develops the angelic dimension of his existence and acquires a strong, heart felt and experienced conviction of the truth and faith that in the beginning he had accepted only superficially.

The principles of Tasawwuf may be listed as follows :

- Reaching substantial, true belief in Divine oneness and living in accordance with its demands.
- In addition to heeding the Divine Speech (the Qur'an), discerning the commands of the Divine Power and Will on the face of the universe (the laws of creation and life which are the subject matter of the sciences) and obeying them.
- Overflowing with Divine love and getting on well with all other beings in the consciousness (originating from Divine love) that the universe is a cradle of brotherhood.
- Acting with a spirit of altruism and therefore giving preference or precedence to the well-being and happiness of others.
- Acting in accordance with the demands of the Divine Will–not with the demands of our own will—and trying

to lead our lives at the 'peaks' of self annihilation in God and subsistence with Him.

- Being open to love, spiritual yearning, delight and ecstasy.
- Acquiring the ability to discern or unveil what is in hearts or minds through the expressions of the face and the Divine mysteries and meanings on the face of events.
- Visiting such places and seeking the company of such people as will encourage avoidance of sin and striving in the way of God.
- Being content with lawful or licit pleasures, and being determined not to take even a single step toward the sphere of the unlawful.
- Continuously struggling against worldly ambitions and the illusions that lead us to suppose this world to be eternal.
- Never forgetting that even in the way of serving religion and striving for the guidance of people to the way of the Truth, salvation is only possible through certainty or conviction (of the truth of religious principles of belief and conduct), sincerity or purity of intention and aiming only to please God.

Acquiring knowledge and understanding of the religious and gnostic sciences, and following the guidance of a perfect spiritual master may be added to these principles, which are of considerable significance in the way of the Sufis.

It may be useful to discuss Tasawwuf in the light of the following basic concepts which are the subject-matter of asceticism, and regarded as the points where one finds the 'Mohammedan Truth' in one's heart. They can also be considered as the lights by which to know and follow the spiritual path of mysticism.

As the history of Islamic religious sciences tells us, the religious commandments are not recorded in the earliest times of Islam. The practice and oral circulation of the commandments pertaining to belief, worship, and daily life enabled people to memorize them. This is why it was not difficult to compile them in books. What had been memorized and practiced was recorded and arranged on paper. In addition, since the religious commandments mentioned above comprise the vital issues in a Muslim's individual and collective life, scholars gave priority to them and compiled books on them. Jurisprudents collected and condified in the form of books the Islamic Law and its rules and principles pertaining to all fields of life. Traditionists established the Prophetic Traditions and way of life and preserved them in books; theologians dealt with the issues concerning Muslim belief, and the interpreters of the Qur'an dedicated themselves to studying the meaning of the Qur'an, including the issues which would later be called the Qur'anic sciences such as Naskh (Abrogation of a law), Inzal (God's sending down the whole of the Qur'an at one time), Tanzil (God's sending down the Qur'an in parts on different occasions), Qiraat (recitation of the Qur'an), and Ta'wil (Exegesis), etc. Thanks to these universally appreciated efforts, the truths of Islam and all its principles were established in a way not to leave any doubt concerning their authenticity.

While all this work was being done in the fields of religious sciences, essentially based on jurisprudence, Tradition (Hadith), theology and Qur'anic interpretation, the Sufi masters who concentrated mostly on the pure spiritual dimension of the Muhammadan Truth tried to draw attention to the essence of man's being, the real nature of existence and the inner dynamics of man and the cosmos, directing attention to the reality of things lying beneath and beyond their outer dimension. Adding to the commentaries on the Qur'an, the narrations of the Traditionists and the deductions of the jurisprudents, their asceticism, spirituality and self purification, in short, their practice and experience of religion, the Sufi masters developed their ways. Thus, the Islamic spiritual life based on the actions of the spirit such as asceticism, regular worship, abstention from all major and minor sins, sincerity and purity of intention, love and yearning and man's admission of his essential impotence and destitution became the subject-matter of a new science called Tasawwuf having its own method, principles, rules and terms. Even if there emerged over time some differences among the orders that were later established, it can be said that the basic subject matter of this science has always been the essence of the Muhammadan Truth.

Unfortunately, it has sometimes occurred that, although they are the two aspects of the same truth, the commandments of Shari'a and Tasawwuf-which is in reality the spirit of Shari'a, comprising austerity, self control and criticism and continuous struggle to resist the temptations of Satan and the carnal, evil commanding self, and fulfil religious obligations, and so on–have been presented as contradictory to each other. While adherence to the former has been regarded as exotericism (self restriction to the outward dimension of religion), following the latter has been seen as pure esotericism. Although this discrimination partly arises from the assertions that the commandments of Shari'a are represented by jurisprudents or muftis, and the other by the Sufis, it should be viewed as (the result of) a natural, human tendency, which is that everyone gives priority to the way more compatible with his temperament and for which he has aptitude.

As jurisprudents, Traditionists and interpreters of the Qur'an produced significant books based on the Qur'an and the Sunna and following the methods dating back to the time of the Prophet ﷺ and the Companions, so also the Sufis compiled books on austerity, spiritual struggle against carnal desires and temptations, states of the spirit and stations depending also on the same sources, with the addition of their own spiritual experiences, love, ardour and rapture. By doing so, they tried to attract the attention of those whom they regarded as restricted to practicing the outward dimension of religion and reflecting only on it, to their way and the spiritual aspect of religious life.

Both the Sufis and the scholars, criticized for being restricted to the outward aspect of religion, aimed to reach God by observing the Divine obligations and prohibitions. Nevertheless, some extremist attitudes occasionally observed on both sides caused some disagreements between them.

Actually there was no substantial disagreement, nor should it have been viewed as a disagreement, that the different aspects and elements of religion were dealt with and presented under different titles. It is by no means a disagreement that while jurisprudence concerns itself with the rules of worship and daily life, with how to regulate and discipline man's individual and social life, Tasawwuf aims to enable man to live his life at a high level of spirituality through self purification and spiritual training. In fact, Tasawwuf and jurisprudence are like the two schools of a university which has undertaken to teach man the two faces or dimensions of Shari'a and educate him to be able to practise it in his life. These two schools cannot be one without the other. One teaches how to perform the prescribed prayers, how to realize the canonical purity required for worship, how to fast, how to give the obligatory alms, and how to regulate his daily life from shopping to marriage, etc. The other concentrates on the meaning of these and other acts of, how to make worshipping an inseparable dimension of man's existence and how to elevate man to the rank of a universal, perfect being, which is the true humanity. That is why neither of these disciplines can be neglected.

Although some impertinent ones among those claiming to be Sufis have gone so far as to label religious scholars as 'scholars of ceremonies' and 'exoterists'., the real, perfected Sufis have always depended on the basic principles of Shari'a and based their thoughts on the Book–Qur'an–and the Sunna, deriving their methods from these basic sources of Islam. The Wasaya ('Advices') and Ri'aya ('Observation of Rules') by al-Muhasibi, al-Ta'arruf li-Madhhabi Ahl al-Tasawwuf ('A Description of the Way of the people of Tasawwuf) by Kalabazi, al-Luma' ('The Gleams') by al-Tusi, Qut al-Qulub ('The Food of hearts') by AbuTalib al-Makki and al-Risala ('The Treatise') by al-Qushayri are among the precious sources where Tasawwuf is dealt with according to the book and Sunna. Among these sources some concentrate on self-control, the purification of the self, while others elaborate various topics concerned with Tasawwuf.

After these great compiliers came Hujjat al-Islam Imam al-Ghazali, the author of ihya' al-Ulum al-Din (Reviving the Religious Sciences'), his most celebrated work. He reviewed all the terms, principles and rules of the way of Tasawwuf and, establishing those agreed on by all the Sufi masters and criticizing others, united once more these two disciplines, namely the outer and inner dimensions of Islam or jurisprudence and Tasawwuf. The Sufi masters coming after him presented Tasawwuf as one of the religious sciences or a dimension thereof, promoting the unity or agreement between themselves and those once called the scholars of ceremonies. In addition, they were able to make some subjects of Sufism like the states of the spirit, certainty or conviction, sincerity and morality, which are dealt with by Tasawwuf more profoundly, a part of the curriculum of madrasas-the institutions where religious sciences are taught.

Although Tasawwuf mostly concentrates on the inner world of man and deals with the religious commandments with respect to their meaning and effects on man's spirit and heart and is therefore abstract, it is not contradictory with any of the Islamic ways based on the Book and the Sunna. Far from being contradictory, it has its source, just like other religious sciences, in the Book and the Sunna and the conclusions the purified scholars of the early period of Islam drew from the Qur'an and the Sunna-ijtihad. It dwells on knowledge, knowledge of God, certainty, sincerity, perfect goodness and other similar, fundamental virtues.

Defining Tasawwuf with different titles such as the science of esoteric truths or of mysteries or the science of man's spiritual states and stations or the science of initiation, does not mean that it is completely different from other religious sciences. Such definitions are the results of experiencing Shari'a throughout centuries by men of different temperaments and dispositions. It is a distortion to present the viewpoints of the Sufis and the thoughts and conclusions of the scholars of Shari'a as essentially different from each other. Although it is an undeniable fact that there have been some Sufis fanatically adherent to their own ways, as well as some religious scholars–jurisprudents, Traditionists, and interpreters of the Qur'an -restricted to the outward dimension of religion, those who follow and represent the middle, straight path have always formed the majority. Therefore, starting from some unbecoming thoughts cherished and words uttered by some jurisprudents and Sufis against each other, it is wrong to conclude that there is a serious disagreement between them. As compared with those always on the side of tolerance and consensus, the numbers of the others who have started or participated in conflict have been very few. This is what is natural, for like the jurisprudents who have depended on the Book and the Sunna in their ways, the Sufis have also depended on these two main sources of Islam.

In addition, the priorities of Tasawwuf have never been different from those of jurisprudence. Both of these ways or disciplines have stressed the importance of belief, doing good deeds and god conduct. The only difference is that, more than the jurisprudents, the Sufis have also focused on purification of the self, deepening in the meaning of good deeds and multiplying them, and attainment of higher standards of good morals, by which man's conscience awakens to knowledge of God and man can enter a way leading to the required sincerity in practicing the religion and obtaining God's good pleasure. Since man can, by means of thee virtues, acquire another nature-another heart-spiritual intellect-within the heart, a deeper knowledge of God, and another 'tongue' to mention God-he can perform all the commandments of Shari'a in a deeper consciousness of, and with a disposition for, servanthood to God, and in greater exhilaration.

It is by means of Tasawwuf that man deepens in spirituality. Through the struggle with the selfhood, through solitude or retreat, invocation, self-control and self-criticism, the veils over the inner dimension of existence are torn apart and, as a result, man gains a strong conviction of the truth of all the major and minor principles of faith. It is essential to discuss in detail the main concepts of islamic mysticism *i.e.*, Sufism. These concepts are as under :

Qalb (Heart) : Qalb is very symbolically used in Islamic mysticism. The term Qalb means heart and heart occupies a central position in the practical esoteric and exoteric aspect of mysticism. If the heart is pure the outward formality of removing the waste of body and mind is said to have been achieved. The seer Patanijali also in his Yoga-sustra put emphasis on the purity of heart. Because of the importance of the symbol the term Qalb carry in it I have given ample space in my discussion, to the term 'Qalb'.

> *"Heart is the home of God, purify it from whatever is other than Him*
>
> *so that the All-Merciful may descend into His palace at nights"*[2].

Regarding the heart we find parallel in the Ishavashyopanishad as under :

> *Isavashyam idam sarvam yat Kim cha jagtyam jagat*
>
> *Tena tyaktena bhunjitaha ma gradhaha kasyashvida*[3]

The Lord is enshrined in the hearts of all. The Lord is the supreme Reality.

> *Rejoice in him through renunciation.*
>
> *Cover nothing. All belongs to the Lord*[4].

Heart has two meanings. One denotes the most vital part of the body which is located in the left part of the chest and resembles a pine cone. With respect to its structure and tissue, heart is different from all other parts of the body. It has two auricles and two ventricles and is the origin of all arteries and veins. Among the parts of the body, it moves by itself, works like a motor and, like a suction pump, pumps blood into the whole of the system.

Heart in Sufi terminology signifies the spiritual aspect of the biological heart as the center of all emotions and intellectual and spiritual faculties such as perception, consciousness, sensation, reasoning and will power. The Sufis call it the human truth, while philosophers, call it the selfhood. Man's real nature consists in heart. With respect to this intellectual and spiritual aspect of his existence, man becomes one knowing, perceiving, and understanding, etc. Spirit is the essence and inner dimension of this faculty. It is heart which God addresses and which undertakes responsibilities, suffers punishment, is rewarded, is elevated through true guidance, abased through deviations, which is honoured or humiliated and is the 'polished mirror' where Divine knowledge reflects.

Heart is of the character which both perceives and is perceived. Man penetrates his soul, corporeal existence and mind by means of it. Heart is like the eye of spirit. Insight may be regarded as its faculty of sight, reason its spirit, and will its inner dynamics.

Heart or, if we may call it so, spiritual intellect has an intrinsic connection with its biological counterpart. The nature of this connection has long been discussed by upanishadic seers and Muslim mystics. Of whatever character this connection may be, it is beyond doubt that there is a close connection between the biological heart and the 'spiritual' one, which is a Divine faculty, the centre of man's true humanity and the source of his feelings and emotions.

What is meant by heart in the Qur'an, religious sciences, morals, literature and Sufism, is the spiritual heart. Belief, knowledge of God, love of God and spiritual deight are the objectives to be achieved through this Divine faculty.

Heart is a luminous, precious ore with two aspects, one looking to the world of spirits and the other to the world of corporeality. If the corporeal existence or physical body of a man is under the direction of spirit, then heart conveys to the body the spiritual effusions of gifts it receives through the world of the spirit and causes it to breathe peace and tranquility.

As stated above, God considers hearts. He treats man according to the quality of his heart. For heart is the stronghold of many elements vital to man's spiritual life and humanity such as reason, knowledge, knowledge of God, intention, belief, wisdom and nearness to God Almight. If heart is alive, then all these elements and faculties are also alive; if, on the contrary, it is caught in diseases, then it is difficult for the elements and faculties mentioned to remain sound. The truthful and confirmed one, upon him be peace and blessings, declares : There is a fleshy part in the body. If it is healthy, then the whole of the body is healthy. If it is corrupted, then all the body is corrupted. Beware! That part is heart. In saying that, he directs attention to the importance of heart for man's spiritual health.

Heart has another aspect or function more important than the others mentioned. It has the points of reliance and seeking help ingrained in it and in man's nature by which shows man to

God as the All–helping and All-Maintaining. That is, it always reminds man of god in the tongues of neediness and seeking help and protection. This is vividly expressed in a saying in words as follows :

> *God said : 'Neither the heavens nor the earth can contain Me.'*
>
> *He is known and recognized as a 'Treasurer' hidden in the heart by the heart itself.*[5]

Man's body is the physical dimension of his existence, while it is heart which constitutes its spiritual dimension. For this reason, it is the direct, eloquent, most articulate, splendid and truthful tongue of knowledge of God and is therefore regarded as more valuable and honoured than the Ka'ba and accepted as the only exponent of the sublime truth that is expressed by the whole of creation to make God known. The Qur'an, by advising us to pray says :

> *Our Lord! Do not cause our hearts to swerve after you have guided us, O God! O Converter of hearts! Establish our hearts firmly on your religion*[6].

This reminds us of the necessity of preserving the heart.

Just as heart can function as a bridge by which all good and blessings may reach man, it can also become a means for man to give an entry permit to all satanic and carnal temptations and all vices. When set on God and guided by Him, it becomes like a projector to diffuse light as far as the remotest, darkest corners of the body, whereas it can become a target for all the poisonous arrows of Satan when put under the command of the carnal self.

Heart is the native home of belief, worship and perfect virtue; a gushing river flowing with the inspirations and radiation arising from the relations between God, man and the universe. Unfortunately, there are innumerable adversaries that try to destroy this world-worthy home, to block this river or divert its course. Among them, hardness (losing the ability to feel and believe), unbelief, conceit, arrogance, worldly ambitions, greed, excessive lusts, heedlessness, selfishness and attachment to status-all these are on the alert to find out the heart's weak spots and destroy it.

Belief is the life of heart, worship is the blood flowing in its veins, and reflection, self supervision and self-criticism are the foundations of its permanence. The heart of an unbelieving one is dead, the heart of a believer who does not worship is in the throes of death, and the heart of a worshipping believer who does not reflect, nor controls himself and accuses himself of his errors and sins, is exposed to all kinds of dangers and diseases. Although the first among these three groups of people carry a 'pump' in their chests, it cannot be said that they have hearts. Those belonging to the second group live in the cloudy or misty atmosphere of their surmises and doubts, they live imprisoned within distances from God, without ever reaching the destination. As for the third group, although they have crossed some distances toward the destination, they are at risk as they have not been able to reach the goal. They advance falteringly, defeat and success follow each other in their struggling in the way of God, and they spend their lives in attempts to climb a 'hill' without being able to get through it.

While, on the other hand, those who have firm belief and live instinct accordance with it as if seeing God and conscious that God oversees them, are in utmost security and under God's protection against faltering and falling. They study existence with insight, penetrate things and discover their reality through the light of God and behave soberly and in self-possession. They tremble with fear of God, between anxieties and hope concerning their end, and they pursue His good pleasure. They try to do whatever they do in way to please God and always live with love of Him. In return, God loves them and causes believing souls also to love them. They are loved and esteemed by men and jinn and receive warm welcome wherever they are.

The truthful hero of *Sura Yusuf,* Prophet Yusuf (Joseph), upon him be peace, is mentioned five times as a man of perfect goodness and deep devotion in the sura called by his name. This means that the whole of creation including the Creator and created, friend and foe, the earth and the heavens, testifies to the strict self-control and self-supervision of Prophet Joseph.

By saying *when Joseph reached his full manhood, we bestowed on him wisdom and knowledge. Thus do we reward those who are perfectly good* (12.22), the Almighty draws attention to the fact that Prophet Joseph was a man of perfect goodness and self-control from when he reached the age of puberty. In the prison he stayed in Egypt, every prisoner whether good or bad discerned the depth of his mind, the purity of his spirit, and appealed to him to solve their problems :

Tell us the interpretation of events, including dreams, for we see you [tobe] among those who are perfectly good (12.36). Joseph succeeded in every trial he has made to undergo and had a place in everyone's heart, friend and foe. Once more God mentions him as a man of perfect goodness, a perfect embodiment of goodness, since he did not change when he was appointed to a high post in the government : Thus we established Joseph in the land, to take possession of it where he pleased. We reach with our mercy whom we will, and we never cause to be lost the reward of those who are perfectly good, [worshipping and acting in consciousness of being always supervised by God] (12.56). When his brothers, who always treated him with envy, acknowledged his goodness and truthfulness before they found out that the minister who was charitable to them in the royal palace of Egypt was Joseph : They said: O exalted sir! He has a father, aged and venerable; so take one of us instead of him, for we see that you are among those who are perfectly good (12.78). Lastly, as a man perfectly matured and having acquired full spiritual contentment, prophet Joseph himself testified to God's blessings on him : God has been indeed gracious to us. Whoever acts in fear of God and full submission to him and is patient, surely God does not waste the reward of those who are perfectly good (12.90).

It is inconceivable that a heart to whose soundness everyone testifies deviates or is deprived of God's blessings. Such a heart has the same meaning with respect to its owner as God's Supreme Throne with respect to the universe and is a polished mirror which the Almighty always views. Such a mirror that the Almighty watches in full appreciation is not something to discard and let break. It is the essence and spirit of human reality and something praised by God.

In the following couplets, mawlana jalal al-Din al-Rumi recalls this :

The Truth says : I consider the heart,
not the form made from water and clay.

You say : I have a heart within me, whereas
the heart is above God's Throne, not below[7]

Tawazzu : (Humility) The meaning of Tawazzu is modesty and humility, the virtue of Tawazzu is the opposite of arrogance, pride and haughtiness. We can interpret it is a man's awareness of his real position before God and behaving both toward God and among people according to that position by seeing himself as one from amongst people and an ordinary, individual part of creation. If a man has been able to convince himself that he is like a threshold of a door or a mat spread on a floor or a pavement stone or a pebble in a stream or chaff and if he can sincerely confess, as Muhammad did. "Everybody else is good but I am bad; everybody else is wheat but I am chaff", then those of the highest stature in the heavens are kissing him on the head. In a narration attributed to the Truthful, Confirmed One, upon him be peace and blessings, it is said : Whoever is humble, God exalts him, and whoever is haughty, God humiliates him. This means that being really great is inversely proportional to behaving as if great, as is being belittled by others to being small.

Some have defined humility as seeing oneself is devoid of all virtues essentially originating in oneself, some others as treating human beings humbly and respectfully in a way deserved by being human, and still others as, unless being honoured by a special Divine treatment, seeing oneself as the worst of mankind. There are still others who define it as the effort to be alert to any stirring in oneself of the ego and suppressing it. Each of these definitions expresses a dimension of humility. Regarding humility I would like to cite examples from the prophetic tradition and Hadith literature as follows :

A Companion sees Caliph 'Umar, may God be pleased with him, carry water in a pitcher on his shoulder and asks : 'What are you about, O Caliph of God's Messenger?' 'Umar, who is one of the foremost in nearness to God, answers : 'Some envoys have come from other countries. I have felt some conceit in my heart and wanted to suppress it.' 'Umar used to cary flour on his back. Once he accused himself while giving sermon from the pulpit and he did not respond to those who criticized him. Like 'Umar, Abu Hurayra carried wood for some time while he was the deputy governor of Madina. When he was the chief judge in madina, Zayd ibn Thabit kissed the hand of ibn 'Abbas, and ibn 'Abbas, known as the interpreter of the Qur'an and the Scholar of the Umma, helped Zayd get on his horse. Hasan, the grandson of the prophet ﷺ (upon him be peace and blessings) sat together with some children who were eating bread crumbs and ate with them. Once Abu Dharr offended Bilal Habashi and in order that Bilal might forgive him, put his head on the ground and said : 'IF THE BLESSED FEET OF Bilal do not tread on this sinful head, it will not rise from the ground.' All these events and many similar others are instances of humility[8].

Both God Almighty and his Messenger emphasized humility so much that one who knows of it feels no doubt that servanthood consists in humility. The Qur'anic expressions, the servants of the All-Merciful are they who walk on the earth in modesty, and if the impudent offend them, they continue their way saying 'Peace!'[9] Praises humility, and the Divine statements, extremely humble toward believers[10] and merciful among themselves. You find them bowing down and falling prostrate[11] are expressions of praise for their ingrained humility reflected in their conduct.

Concerning humility, the glory of mankind also declares :

God has ordered me that you must be humble and that no one must boast to another.

Shall I inform you of one whom Hellfire will not touch? Hellfire will not touch one who is near to God and amiable with people, and mild and easy to get on with.

God exalts one who is humble. That one sees him so small but he is truly great in the sight of people.

O God! Make me see myself as small.[12]

The Glory of Mankind, upon him be peace and blessings, lived as the most humble of people.

- He stopped at the places where children were, and played with and greeted them.
- If someone held him by the hand and wanted to lead him somewhere, he never objected.
- He helped his wives with housework.
- When people were working, he worked together with them.
- He mended his shoes and clothes, milked sheep and fed animals.
- He sat at the table with his servant.
- He always welcomed the poor warmly.
- He looked after windows and orphans.
- He visited the ill, followed funerals and answered the call of the slaves in the community.

The beloved servants of God, from God's Messenger, upon him be peace and blessings, to Caliph 'Umar from him to numerous saints, purified and perfected scholars, and those honored with nearness to God, have held that the sign of greatness in the great is humility and modesty, while the signs of smallness in the small is arrogance and vanity, and they aimed hereby to guide people to the way of becoming perfect men.

True humility is that a man must know what his worth really can be before God's infinite Grandeur and make this an ingrained, essential part of his nature. Those who have been able to make this their second nature are humble and balanced in their relations with others. For those who have realized their nothingness before God Almighty are always balanced in both their religious lives and their relations with people.

They obey the commandments of religion, for they have no problems with either the revealed truths of religion or its matters related to human reason. They have conviction of the truth of whatever is declared in the Qur'an and the authentic Traditions of the Prophet ﷺ (upon him be peace and blessings.) If something declared in the Qur'an or related from the Prophet ﷺ through reliable channels of transmission seems to them as if contradictory with human reason or established rational or scientific facts, they do not attempt to object to them and try to learn the truth of the matter. For this reason, it is nonsense of those devoid of humility and modesty to assert that if there is a contradiction between reason or rational premises and the revealed and narrated principles of religion, reason or what is rational is preferred. Also, the assertion that judgements drawn by reasoning and analogy must be given priority over the revealed principles is a deviation. The wonders worked and spiritual pleasures felt in the ways other than the way of the Prophet ﷺ upon him be peace and blessings, mean God's inciting one working those wonders or feeling those pleasures to perdition because of his sins through such 'successes.'

Those who have achieved humility are completed convinced of the truth of whatever the Prophet ﷺ communicated to people and never think otherwise. They try to practice it in their lives and if something else for example, a wise saying or a great accomplishment, allures them to itself as if more beautiful or acceptable, they accuse themselves of being unable to discern the incomparable superiority of the revealed truths and expressions, saying :

> *There are many people who find fault with the words having no defects.*
> *However, the fault lies in their defective understanding.*

They are certain that it is impossible to be prosperous in the other world by following the ways opposing the Qur'an and the Sunna. They find the greatest source of power in servanthood to God. In reality, one who worships God never lowers himself to adore anybody except the Allah. How apt the following words of Bedi-uz-zaman are :

> *Do not see anything or anybody else other than God as so much greater than you as to deserve adoration or servant hood. Nor boast of yourself in a way to see yourself as greater than others. As creatures are equal in being distant from being worshipped, so also are they equal in that they are all created.*

Those who are truly humble do not attribute to themselves the fruits of their work and efforts, nor do they regard as a cause of superiority over others their successes or the efforts they have exerted in the way of God. They are not attracted to people's good opinion of themselves and never demand a return for other services in the way of God. Regarding their being loved by others as a sincerity test, they do not exploit God's favours on them as a means of boasting to others.

In short, just as humility is the portal to good conduct or being characterized with the qualities of God (such as generosity, merciful, helpful, forgiving, etc.), it is also the first and foremost means of being near to both the created and the Creator. Roses grow on earth. Man was created on the earth not in the heavens. The time when a believer is nearest to God is when he is prostrate before Him. While recounting the Prophet's Ascension to the heavens, the Qur'an refers to him as his (God's) servant, as a sign of his humility and utmost modesty.

Qabd and Bast

Qabd (strain) and bast (expansion), which almost everyone feels at times during his life, relates especially to those who live their lives consciously.

Literally meaning being caught, being in straits or distressed and being grasped by hand, qabd (strain) in the language of Sufism means that the link between a man and the source of his spiritual gifts and radiance is cut for a certain period with the result that he feels distressed, suffers from spiritual obstruction and 'constipation.' While bast (expansion) can be described as extension, distension, development, relief and being freed from spiritual 'constipation,' and inwardly or spiritually developing to the point that the seeker becomes a means of mercy in existence and embraces all things or beings.

Fear and hope or expectation are each a deliberate attitude and a first station for a traveller on the way to the Truth. Strain and expansion are a mysterious 'bargain' without the will or intention of the traveller, one blocking his way and the other making him taking wings to fly to the heights.

If fear and hope are an anxiety about and a joy of expectation relating to the future and liked and disliked things, strain and expansion can be regarded as the heart's contracting with gloom and depression and beating with joy.

Strain and expansion have the same meaning for those who travel on the slopes of knowledge of God as fear and hope or expectation have for the newly initiated.

Strain and expansion are in the hands of God even if we cannot exclude from them some part of man's free will, which is of only a nominal nature : God straitens and expands (2.245). As the whole of existence is in His grasp and free disposal, it is he who directs and disposes however; He wishes all things from heavens to the human heart. The Prophetic saying, Heart is between the two Fingers of the All-Merciful. He turns it from state to state and gives it whatever form' He wishes, reminds us of this fact.

When God wills, He contracts a heart so tightly and makes it suffer for want of such things that no one other than Him can satisfy it. By contrast, he expands and exhilarates it to such an extent that it needs nothing.

The majesty of God causes strain, while expansion is by his Grace. While Grandeur and magnificence relating to God's manifesting all His Names of existence are displayed in the former, mercy manifests in the latter. In the former, there is the frightening, awesome, and majestic nature of the Power which turns all existence from huge systems to particles, while in the latter there are affectionate breezes to the spirits which tremble with the awe of this infinitely vast, overwhelming power, this overpowering majesty.

Not everyone can feel such manifestations of majesty and Grace at the same level. The extent of strain and expansion is proportionate to the emotional and spiritual capacity of people. Naturally, what an ordinary one feels in the name of distress and relief or rejoicing is not of the same degree as the spiritual joy and anxieties of one awakened to Divine truths who is continuously on the alert for what will come through the half opened door from the realms beyond and conscious of the fact that he is incessantly overseen from above.

Like everything else and every occurrence in existence, strain and expansion are at the disposal of the Creator and continuously alternate like nights and days. Even if there may be causes of this alternation originating from the deeds man does out of his free will, Divine Will extends or shortens the periods of strain and expansion and throws man into tensions or makes him overflow with delight. There are times when a man covers a long span of time as if flying like birds without being caught in strain, while there are other times when strain visits him too frequently and the periods of strain persist to the extent that he feels as if rolling from one pit into another and is exposed to great distresses.

As it causes strain that one neglects to fulfil what one must do as required by the spiritual position bestowed on him by God, sins usually bring strain along with themselves. For this reason, a believer must always be on the alert (against committing new sins and deviations) while suffering strain. He must be careful lest heedlessness should overpower him, and he must try to be cleansed of sins through sincere repentance and good deeds. Once more, he must stand in waiting for what will come from the realms beyond.

While strain is accompanied by fear, perplexity and feelings of spiritual emptiness, expansion manifests itself in the forms of joy, ecstasy and some feelings or utterance of pride. For this reason, expansion may be risky for spiritually[7] less-developed ones who have not yet been able to attune themselves to the conditions of journeying in 'celestial' realms. Although there are also some risks of strain, the risks of expansion are greater and more in number. For one caught in strain usually feels in his conscience that he is absolutely in need of the Almighty and turns to Him in sincere acknowledgment of his destitution. He entreats, 'Hold me! Hold me lest I should fall!' and, escaping the spiritual waste he feels, he is favoured with the Almighty's help and reaches the heights which he cannot reach in times of expansion. It is because of this that while some people are exposed to heedlessness and loss of spiritual energy in times of expansion, strain serves to lead almost every one to alertness. In addition to this, the strain originating from some of our sins or neglect usually becomes the beginning of a new wave of expansion; similarly, the expansion which causes pride and loss of spiritual energy may give rise to new strains.

A true believer is one who can judge each of his state as it really is with all its aspects and make it fruitful.

Strain and expansion are each a manifestation from him for one who knows the Reality.

He expands so that the servant should thank Him and strains so that he should be more sharpened.

Dahsha & Khayrat (Astonishment & Surprise)

Every traveller journeying in the valleys of love and zeal sometimes burns with love and sometimes overflows with joy owing to the wine of immortality offered by the Beloved. While burning, he sighs, 'O Cup-bearer, I have burnt away. Give me some water!' While he is looking attentively through the door of the Beloved left ajar, he entreats, 'I have dipped my finger into the honey of love. Give me some water!' So long as the traveller cannot be saved from worldly anxieties and considerations of distance or, in other words, until he goes beyond the spheres of the manifestations of Names and Attributes to be honoured with the manifestation of Divine Essence, he continues to travel between burning and entreating and having his lot from the pure drink the Lord offers. He continues to pursue more and more knowledge of God. Every new Divine gift increases his desire, and as his desire increases, new gifts pour into his breast. He embroiders his knowledge of God with his feelings and thoughts travelling between his heart and things. Like a honeybee collecting nectar from flowers and thereby causing flowers to be the source of honey, he collects the nectar of knowledge of God from the manifestations of Divine names and Attributes that open like flowers in the garden of the universe. He distills the nectar he collects through the skill of his appreciative and grateful conscience and feels as if his sight had reached the rays of the Attributes themselves. Then he dreams of reaching the Divine being himself and is striken with astonishment. The writer of Gulistan ('The Rose Garden') expresses the traveller's feelings of astonishment and amazement as he burns and takes drink :

At times You show Your Beautiful Face but it is veiled without being completely seen,

Thus You incite us to compete to be able to see You and increase our fire.

When I see unveiled the Beloved with Whom I have fallen in love.

something occurs to me and I am bewildered on my way.

The Beloved lights a fire in my breast and then puts it out with a drizzle.

That is why you find me burnt away and drowned in an ocean.

Ismail Haqqi Bursawi presents travellers as incessantly intoxicated Sunken in the love of the Lord :

All saintly ones are intoxicated with the pure water their Lord offers them (76.21);

Seven, five and four are intoxicated with His Beautiful Face.

If the traveller has not been able to prepare his heart according to both the requirements of his spiritual journeying and the commandments of Shari'a, that is, if he does not think and reason in the light of Prophethood while his feelings fly in the boundless realm of his spiritual state, he will inevitably fall; he will be confused and bewildered, speaking and acting against to the spirit of Shari'a.

Jami' expresses astonishment and amazement in his vivid language :

The women of Egypt were astounded and cut their hands when they saw the beauty of Joseph. O Master! If they had seen your beauty, they would have trust the daggers in their hands into their breasts. Speaking of Joseph's beauty where your beauty is mentioned means no more than telling tales.

If transient, wordly beauties and perfections that are only the reflections through many veils of the Infinitely Perfect and Beautiful One, can seduce man, it will not be possible for us to perceive the dazzling awe and amazement produced by beholding and gazing upon that Beauty.

Those who prefer to serve faith and the Qur'an in this age should not aim at all the pleasures, whether bodily or spiritual, and continue their service aided by God in awe of and with amazement at the extent God comes to their aid and makes them successful. They should never conceive of anything other than serving Islam. This is a special gift of amazement to the army of light from God's special treasury of which We make the distribution among the people, of the path.

Shawq & Ishtiyaq (Gleeful Zeal & Yearning)

Literally meaning strong desire, excessive wishing, joy emanating from knowing, delight and longing, shawq (joyful zeal) in the language of sufism, expresses the overflowing of the heart with the desire to meet with the Beloved Who cannot be comprehended and vanishes after being 'observed.' Some have described it as a joyful desire, excitement and longing which a lover excessively feels in his heart to see the Face of the beloved, while some others have regarded it as a fire burning to ashes all the desires, wishes, yearning and inclinations other than those felt to meet with the beloved.

Gleeful zeal or shawq originates in love. The remedy of a heart burning with longing to meet with the beloved is meeting with him, and shawq is a wing of light to be able to meet with Him. When a lover finds his beloved, his zeal disappears, while yearning for him (ishtiyaq) increases more and more. One who yearns for Him never stops yearning and, whenever he is favored with some special manifestations of His Essence, he wishes more. It is for this reason that the Prince of the Prophets and the Greatest of Mankind, upon him be peace and blessings, who, equipped at each moment with a new radiance of knowledge and love of God and spiritual delight, incessantly traveled between the summits of love, joyful zeal and yearning, used to pray to him, saying; O God! I ask You for zeal to observe your perfectly beautiful Face and meet with, You.

In interpreting the Qur'ans statement, those who believe are firmer in love of God, some interpreters of the Quran remark :

Joyful zeal is felt toward the things partly perceivable and partly incomprehensible. It is felt toward the things neither completely comprehensible nor completely incomprehensible. A man feels no zeal toward the things that he has never seen nor heard of nor knows nothing about. Nor does he feel interest in the things which he completely comprehends or perceives. Zeal and yearning can be divided into two categories :

The first is the yearning produced by the separation from the beloved after meeting with and gazing upon Him. The sighs that the flute of Mawlana Jalal al-Din al-Rumi uttered and the creaking, painful sounds which Yunus heard from the revolving water-wheel are the groans coming from the separation from the Beloved after the togetherness in the past eternity. They will continue until the final union or meeting with Him.

The second is of the kind that a lover sees his Beloved from behind a veil without completely comprehending Him. He feels his presence but cannot see him. He dips his finger into the honey of love but is not allowed to take a new step further. Since he has to consume with thirst, his cries, 'I am consuming away with thirst, give me some water! do not get any answer.

The spirit of man observed him in an assembly of past eternity where God made all human beings testify of themselves, saying, 'Am I not your Lord? and they answered, 'Yes, assuredly. We testify! After this assembly, either because his being a human being required it to be so or because he would have to be tested and believe in Him without seeing Him, man was thrown into the pangs of a temporary separation. This is why he always dreams of him in conscious or unconscious longing for him and burns with a yearning to re-unite with Him. What is more significant than this is the yearning which the most Sacred Being feels toward pure, innocent and unadulterated souls in a way appropriate for his essential independence of all being. It may be this Divine eagerness which is the real source of the yearning which enters the hearts of men.

Zeal is turning to the beloved with all one's inward and outward feelings and shutting oneself from all appetites other than those felt to meet with Him. As for yearning, it means one's overflowing with the desires and wishes related to Him. Both zeal and yearning are two of the sources from which spirit is fed. Both of them are painful but exhilarating and wearisome, and distressing but promising.

There is none else among human beings more in anguish but happier than him who burns with love and groans with zeal. Such a one becomes so angelic when he is enraptured with the thought and hope of meeting with God that if he were offered paradise at that time, he would not enter it. He burns inwardly with the pangs of separation to such a degree that even the waters of paradise could not extinguish the fire in his heart until he meets with the Supreme Friend. Paradoxically, he never thinks of escaping that fire. Let alone thinking of escaping it, even if the palaces of Paradise were to prevent him from burning with the fire of his zeal to meet with the Supreme Friend, he would utter such cries as resembling the cries that the people of Hell would raise to be saved from Hell-fire.

Worldly people cannot know what that zeal means and the state of those who have it. People of zeal feel amazed at worldly people being engrossed in worldly affairs and pleasures. Their amazement is quite natural, for God Almighty told the prophet David, upon him be peace : O David! If those who love and show inclination to the world knew how much I care about them and like them to resist against sins and how I expect to meet with human beings, they would be dying with the zeal to meet with Me.

When the zeal to meet with God invades a lover's being, he overflows with the feelings of pain and delight and cries :

Zeal has bewildered-me; zeal has burnt me.
Zeal has intervened between sleep and my eyes.
Zeal has invaded me; zeal has engrossed me.
Zeal has overwhelmed me; zeal has stricken me with awe.

This degree of zeal sometimes incites the lover to stand up and dance or turn round. The lover should be excused for such movements, as he cannot resist the spiritual state in which he is :

Say to him who wants to prevent a man of ecstasies from going into ecstasies :

"You have not tasted the wine of love together with us, so leave us!"

When souls overflow with the zeal to meet with the Beloved.

Know, O you unaware of spirituality that bodies begin to dance.

O guide, who incites lovers, stand up and move us with the name of the beloved and breathe life into us.

In the way to be preferred today for the service of the faith and the Qur'an, a way based on acknowledgment of one's poverty and impotence before God's Wealth and Power, and on thankfulness and zeal, zeal means always being hopeful and continuing the service without being dispirited and showing loss of energy. It also means thinking that there is an aspect of Divine mercy even in the most distressing and reverse conditions and waiting for God's help and victory in utmost reliance on him.

Ashq (Passion or Intense, Ecstatic Love)

'Ashq' means intense love and fondness felt for perfection, beauty or physical charm. This sort of love is usually called 'figurative or metaphorical love–love for the opposite sex' by the Sufis. The real love is love of the Eternal monarch which is felt for His Grace and Beauty manifested within his Majesty and for His Majesty manifested within His Grace and Beauty.

The real, intense love felt for God is a wing of light granted to us by Him to reach him. Feeling such a love can be described as the spirit being like a moth drawn toward the Light which is the essence of existence. This intense love or 'Ashq is the most basic and mysterious cause of the creation of the universe. God has created the universe since He desired to be known and loved and also for the reason that the souls awakened to truth would feel and manifest a deep interest in His Essence, Attributes and Names. 'Ashq which spirit feels without the intervention of man's free will cannot be controlled by man himself. Its real source is God Himself Who loves Himself in a way special to His Sacred

Essence and essential independence of the created and which is essentially different from the lover the created feel for the created or the Creater. This sacred, essential love of God for Himself including his Attributes and Names is the reason why God has created the universe and why mankind appeared in the world. It manifests in man as love of God as the most essential centre of relationship with God.

Ashq is the final point of the steps leading to God. It can be said that a lover who has reached this point has no further steps to take following it. God manifested Himself first as this sacred, essential love which is required by His being God. This love must in no way be confused with or taken as the kind of love man feels for either the created or the Creator himself. Since there is no other word more appropriate to express it, I feel obliged to use the word 'love. However, some tend to describe as knowledge this first manifestation of God, which is regarded as God's aloofness to be known. This aloofness is called Knowledge on account of its being God's manifesting His Knowledge, Sacred Love on account of its being God's loving to observe and be 'observed', the Tablet on account of its comprehending or containing the whole of existence, and the Pen on account of its handling all things in existence in all their details. Jabarut (The highest, immaterial Empyrean) and the Truth of Ahmad the Prophet's Name mentioned in the original of the Gospels and in the heavens) are other titles of this condenscension or God's first manifestation. The Sacred Love is a mystery special to the Divine Essence. Other Attributes of His are appended to or dependent on this Love It is for this reason that those who fly with the wings of 'Ashq reach direct to the Divine Essence and attain to Amazement. Others have to pass through the intermediate realms of the worlds of things.

The ways leading to God are almost uncountable. Tasawwuf or the sciences of truth are the food, light and other necessities of the journeying that the wayfarers need along those ways, and the (spiritual) orders (tariqas) are the ports from which they set out or the schools where the principles of the journeying are taught.

Those ways leading to the Truth can be divided into two main categories :

The first is the way where the wayfare is offered or taught such principles as eating less, drinking less, sleeping less, more contemplation and restraining from unnecessary social intercourse. Almost all of the Sufi orders are based upon this way. The main invocations recited by its followers are the Seven Names, which are : There is no God but God, God, he, the Truth, the All Living, the Self Subsistent, and the All-Overwhelming. By reciting these names it is intended to pass through the seven steps of the carnal soul which are the Evil Commanding Soul, the Self Condemning Soul, the Soul Having Inspiration, the Soul at Rest, the Soul Well-Pleased, the Soul Pleasing (to God), and the Purified or Innocent Soul. To the seven Names mentioned some add such Names of Majesty as the All-Powerful, the All-Strong, the All-Compelling, the Master, and the All-Loving, and some others such Names of Grace as the Unique, the One, the Peerlessly All-Single, and the Eternally Besought-of-All.

The other way is based on strict obedience to the Book–the Qur'an and the Sunna and encouragement of certain recitations. Those who follow this way try their utmost to comply with the Sunna in whatever they do. Rather than reciting certain Names, they pursue the way God's Messenger worshipped, invoked, and prayed to God, meditated on His acts and creatures and mentioned Him with all His Names. Together with meticulously following the commandment of Sharia, they are firmly attached to their guides or teachers and abandon themselves to the tides of 'ashq' and (spiritual) attraction toward God. Once they have attained 'ashq and attraction, existence with its outer dimension vanishes from their sight. They annihilate them selves and begin to feel and observe the absolute Divine Unity. This is the point where they immediately come to their senses without getting into confusions and going to extremes regarding the relationship between the Creator and the created, and thus complete their journeying.

The basic principles of this second way are regular worship, love, spiritual attraction toward God, regular recitation and the companionship of the guide or teacher. What we mean here by recitation includes, besides mentioning God with all His Names, study or classes of whatever serves to lead to God. This is what the Prophet ﷺ, upon him be peace and blessings, meant in his description of the group of people with whom God is pleased, by saying : They make studies together.

Mahabba (Love)

Mahabba (love) means fondness, tender and kind feelings, and inclination. When love affects and invades all feelings of man, it is called passion and when it gets as deep and irresistible as to burn with the desire of union, it is called fervour and enthusiasm. Love has been defined by the Sufis as the relation of the heart with the Truly Beloved One or the irresistible desire felt for Him, or trying to comply with His desires or Commandments in all one's acts and thoughts, or being enraptured and intoxicated without 'sobriety' until the time of union. All these definitions can be summed up as 'standing' in the Presence of God and being freed from all transient relationships and worries.

True love means that a lover is set wholly on the Beloved and is always and inwardly with Him, and that he always feels Him and is freed from all other kinds of desires and wishes. The heart of him who has such a degree of love always beats with a new consideration for the Beloved at every moment, his imagination always travels in His mysterious climate, his feelings receive new messages from Him at every moment and his will takes wings with these messages and he passionately desires to meet Him.

While a lover who transcends his self with the wings of love and reaches his Lord at the point of passion and enthusiasm carries out his responsibilities toward the King of his heart, his heart is set on His vision. His nature is 'burned' with the lights of Divine Grandeur and lost in wonder and amazement. With the cup of love on his lips, while the veils of the Unseen are lifted before him one after the other, he is intoxicated with study of the meanings coming in rays from behind those veils and enraptured with the pleasure of watching the scenes behind them. He walks by the command of God, the Truth, and stops likewise by His command. When he speaks he does so by the inspirations coming from Him, and when he keeps silent, he does so in His name. Sometimes he is on a journeying toward Him, sometimes is in 'His Company,' and sometimes is occupied with communicating His message to others.

Some have defined love as doing good and favour when it is used as God's love of His distinguished servants, and as obedience, devotion and unconditional submission when it is used as a servant's love of God. The following couplets of Rabia al-'Adawiya are significant in expressing this meaning :

You talk about loving God while you disobey Him;
I swear by my life that this is something very strange..
If you were truthful in your love, you would obey Him,
For a lover obeys whom he loves.

Love is based on two important pillars :

- The first is that which is manifested by the lover's acts. A lover tries to comply with the Beloved's desires.
- The second relates to the inner world of the lover, who should inwardly be closed to everything else unrelated to Him. True men of God mean this when they talk about love. According to them, emotional concern with or love of any kind of pleasure including spiritual ones or interest cannot be called love in its true sense. It can only be figurative love.

Every lover cannot feel the same degree of love for the Beloved. Love varies according to the spiritual and emotional depth of the lover and the degree of his consciousness and care in his obedience to the Beloved.

1. The love felt by those who are yet at the beginning of the way is not established and constant. They dream of being able to acquire the rank of Perfect Goodness and can at times receive some signs of Knowledge of God. There are times when they thrill at the twinkle of the 'lights' appearing on their horizon and vaguely feel amazement and wonder.

2. Those who have taken a long way fly in the heaven of love toward the highest point. They live in the bright climate of the Qur'an as embodiments and examples of the good morals of the Prophet Muhammad ﷺ (upon him be peace and blessings.) While trying to represent the good morals of the Prophet ﷺ, they are never in expectation of any reward material or spiritual and demand no pleasure. Even at the summit of his holy representation, like fruit-bearing trees whose branches bend with the weight of their fruits, they lower their wings of humility and always mention the Beloved. If they are shaken with a fault or error, they severely criticize their selves and fight with them.
3. Those that are the most advanced in love of God are like rain clouds in the 'heaven' of Islam. They feel existence by Him and live with Him, seeing and breathing by Him. In a never-ending, never-stoping cycle, they are filled with the pangs of separation (from Him) and the desire of meeting with Him, and when relieved or emptied, they mount on a light and descend to earth to embrace the whole existence animate or inanimate.

In whatever degree of love, one who turns to Him with heart felt desires and sincere enthusiasm, gets his reward according to the depth of his feelings and concern with Him. The first of those three groups mentioned above receive special favour and mercy, while those of the second group reach the horizon of perceiving the Attributes of grace and Majesty, being freed from defects of character. Those of the third group are illumined by the lights of His Being and awakened to the reality of things, getting in touch with the dimension of existence behind veils. That is, the Almighty manifests the lights of His Grandeur to burn up the attributes of those whom He loves coming from their corporeality and 'elevate' them to the realm of Divine Attributes such as the All-Seeing and All-Hearing. He makes them fully awakened to the fact that they are poor and helpless before Him by themselves and fills their hearts with the lights of the existence of the Divine Being.

A lover with such degree of love, and who is rewarded with so much Divine favour, attains to an eternal life which cannot be described in terms of either existence or non existence. Like a bar of iron put into fire and therefore seen as if a bar of fire, he may not be able to distinguish the Divine Being and His manifestations and therefore expresses his feelings and experiences in terms associated with such false beliefs as incarnation and union (with God). Whereas in such circumstances, what must be taken into consideration is the established criteria of the Sunna. The expressions uttered by men of profound spirituality lost in love of God while they are intoxicated with love cannot be taken as criteria to judge them. Otherwise we may be feeling enmity toward such friends of God who are favoured with continuous 'company' of God according to the prophetic Tradition.

A man is with him whom he loves, and, as declared in the Hadith Qudsi, whoever becomes an enemy of my friends has waged war on me, we have waged ware on god the Almighty.

Ma'rifa (Spiritual Knowlege of God)

Literally meaning skill, talent, a special capacity particular to certain people, means and knowing by means of something, ma'rifa, according to the travellers on the path of God, is the rank where knowing is united with the one who knows and becomes second nature to him and every state of him reveals what or who is known. Some have defined ma'rifa as the appearance and development of knowledge of God in one's conscience, or knowing God by one's conscience, which means man's self-realization or his rising to the point where he has realized his humanity with all its intrinsic values and dimensions. This may be what is meant by 'the one who knows himself know his Lord'.

The first rank of ma'rifa consists in discerning the manifestations of the Divine Names surrounding us on all sides and travelling in the amazing climate of the Attributes behind the door of mystery half-opened through these manifestations. During this travelling, lights flow continuously from the eyes and ears of the traveller on the path of the Truth to his tongue, and his heart begins to direct his acts which serve as if a tongue confirming and proclaiming the Truth. This tongue becomes, so to speak, a diskette of 'good words' and various lights from light giving truth of Unto Him good words ascend, and the righteous deed causes them to rise[13] begin to be reflected on the screen of his conscience. A man who has acquired such a degree of ma'rifa is closed to all kinds of evils and enveloped by the breezes blowing from the realms beyond. Corridors of light are opened from his spirit toward the One known by the heart–as *Ibrahim Haqqi* stated it allegorically : God said : 'I can be contained by neither the heavens nor the earth.' He is known by the heart as if a hidden treasure in the heart and man is enraptured with the pleasures of observing such scenes that he does not think of returning to his normal life.

This point where a traveller to the Truth is completely closed to all else save God and has resolved against all kinds of corporeal desires and impulses, letting himself be carried by the tides of peace, is the point of ma'rifa. One who travels around this point is called a traveller to ma'rifa, while another who has reached it, is called an 'arif (gnostic or one who has spiritual knowledge of God).

The difference between the commentaries made on ma'rifa arises from the differences of either temperaments or schools of thought or the levels of Gnostics. Some have sought ma'rifa in the Gnostics themselves and thought the feeling of awe observed in them as the manifestation of ma'rifa, others have seen it connected with serenity and judged the former's depth according to the latter's profundity; while still others have regarded it as the hearet's being completely closed to all else save God. There are still those who have interpreted it as the wonder and admiration that the heart feels amidst the tides of Divine manifestations. The hearts of those always beat with wonder and amazement, their eyes open and close with amazement, and their tongues pronounce with wonder and admiration, I acknowledge that I am unable to praise you as You praise Yourself.

With the spirit always flying upward toward eternity, and the heart enraptured with the pleasures of finding peace or being at rest but always self-possessed and cautious, life in the climate of ma'rifa is as calm and peaceful as in the gardens of Paradise. Side by side or coping with angels, those who have acquired ma'rifa are included in the meaning of They do not disobey God in whatever He commands them and carry out what they are commanded (66.6). With feelings like buds waiting for day time to open, those souls fully open with ma'rifa in day time and experience the pleasure of intimacy with Him at every moment with a new dimension of ma'rifa. So long as they keep their eyes fixed on the door of the Truth, they are intoxicated with coming together with Him a few times every day or even every hour and enraptured with a new manifestation at every moment.

While those supposing themselves to be scholars continue to 'crawl,' and philosophers to philosophize, advancing on the information they have with great difficulties, an 'arif (gnostic–one who has acquired ma'rifa) always tastes peace and talks about peace in a prism of light. Even at the times when he is shaken with fear and awe of the Almighty, he feels infinite pleasure and, while his eyes weep, his heart smiles.

There are some differences of manners and tendencies among Gnostics coming from the differences of temperaments and schools of spiritual training. While some are, like whirlpools, deep and silent, and it is difficult to identify them among people because of their simple, quiet appearance, others 'gurgle' like waterfalls. There are some who always and restlessly seek for fear of committing sins and being unable to do a single good thing and are never tired of praising their Lord, while others continuously travel in the climate of awe, modesty and familiarity and never think of leaving this 'ocean.' There are still others who are like earth which everybody else 'treads' -no one pays any respect to them or thinks that they are Gnostics-and others who, like clouds, send 'water' to everyone under them, and others who, like breezes, tough our feelings and blow us good and favour.

There are some signs to recognize a gnostic. A gnostic expects favour from and becomes intimate with no one else other than the Known One. He lifts his eyelids and the doors of his heart to no one other than Him. The turning of a true gnostic with love to and his desiring any one else other than Him is the greatest suffering for him. One who has not been able to acquire true knowledge of God Almighty cannot distinguish between the Beloved and others, and one who has not been able to have intimacy or privacy with the Beloved cannot know the torment and pain of separation.

Dhikr (Recitation of God's Names)

Literally meaning mentioning, remembrance and recollection, according to the Sufis, Dhikr denotes regular and periodical recitation of one or some of God's Names in the same session of recitation. Some spiritual Sufi orders prefer to recite God–the proper Name of the Divine Being–while some others There is no god but God–the declaration of Divine unity–and still others one or a few of the other Names according to the choice of the master of the order.

Like thankfulness, Dhikr is also a duty of servanthood to be performed both verbally and actively and also by heart and other faculties of conscience. Verbal Dhikr ranges from mentioning God Almighty with all His Beautiful Names and sacred Attributes and praising, exalting and glorifying him and proclaiming one's helplessness and destitution before Him in the tongue of prayer and supplication, to reciting His Book and following it and voicing His signs in nature and the seal special to Him on each thing and event. Dhikr by the faculties of conscience, primarily including the heart, comprises reflecting on the proofs of His existence and Unity and His Names and Attributes radiating in the book of creation; meditating on the commandments His orders and prohibitions and His promises and threats and His rewarding and punishment issuing from His Lordship to design or order our lives; trying to penetrate the mysteries lying behind the veil of visible existence by both studying creation and following certain spiritual disciplines; repeatedly observing the heavenly beauties manifested as a result of such instances of penetration; and thinking that whatever exists in the universe from galaxies to atoms pulses with messages from the high empyrean world, manifesting the meaning of the invisible world and functioning as a window to discern the Truth of the Truths. Those who are able to feel existence constantly pulsing, and the invisible world speaking eloquently, and observe the manifestations of grace and Majesty through those windows, are so enraptured with such spiritual pleasure as neither eyes have seen nor ears have heard, that an hour or life spent with these pleasures is equal to hundreds of years, and they advance along their way to eternity lost in Divine gifts and spiritual delights. At the point where the one reciting feels the lights of His Glorified Face surrounding all existence, he is rewarded with the seeing of indescribable scenes and, coming to be aware of all other beings reciting God's Names each in its own tongue, he finds himself mentioning Him with many of His Names.

There are times when recitation of God's Names leads the one rediating into a trance like state where he loses himself. In this entranced state or ecstatic contemplation, some utter, "There is no existent save He," some others, "There is nothing seen save He," and still others, "There is no God but God," and there are some who, meaning and keeping in mind all of the Divine names according to the inclusiveness of their consciousness, pronounce only save God and continue to pronounce the declaration of God's Unity.–Anal-Haq

The seconds spent in such an atmosphere of nearness to God and His Company the seconds of light and radiance are much happier and more rewarding than the years spent with no light with respect to eternal life. This is what is referred to in saying attributed to the Prophet ﷺ, upon him be peace and blessings; I have a time with my God when neither any angel nearest to God nor any Prophet sent as Messenger can compete with me.

Active recitation or recitation by the body consists in practicing religion with utmost care, doing all the obligations enthusiastically and refraining from prohibitions consciously. Profundity and awareness in verbal recitation largely depend on this kind of recitation, that is, the active one, which also means knocking on the door of Divinity and searching the ways to be admitted to the Divine Court and, proclaiming one's helplessness and destitution, taking refuge in Divine Power and Wealth.

One who regularly and intensively mentions God or recites one or some of His Names is taken under the protection of God and supported by Him as if having made a contract with Him. The verse, Remember and mention Me, and I will remember and mention you[14] expresses this degree of recitation by which man's innate destitution becomes the source of wealth and helplessness the source of power.

The verse above means; if you remember and mention God and worship Him regularly, He will return it with His favours and bounties. If you invoke Him and supplicate to Him, He will pour out His favours on you. If you do not forget Him because of your worldly affairs and preoccupations, He will remove the obstacles on your way in both this world and the next. You will always feel His Company when you are alone, and He will befriend you when you are left alone and need friendship. You will always remember and mention Him when you are at ease and comfort, and He will have mercy on you when you encounter troubles and suffer pains. You will struggle in His way to spread His Name all over the world, and He will save you from humiliation in both the world here and the Hereafter. You will be sincere in your endeavours in His way, and He will honour you with such special favours and ranks that neither eyes have ever seen nor ears heard nor hearts conceived of. The desire to mention Him and recite His Names will be rewarded with Divine help to be able to do that and increase in guidance. The continuation of the verse mentioned above. Give thanks to me and do not show ingratitude to me[15] suggests a virtuous circle in which a believer passes from recitation to thankfulness and from thankfulness to recitation.

Recitation is the essence of all kinds or acts of worship and the origin of this essence is the holy Qur'an. Then come the luminous, celebrated words of the Prophet ﷺ, to whom the Islamic Shari'a was sent.

With all its aspects or sorts mentioned above, recitation, whether it be done loudly or silently, is an action to attract and embody the manifestations of the lights of God's Glorified 'Face.'

Recitation also denote proclaiming God to all men and Jinn and spreading His Name all over the world as thankfulness for His manifest and hidden favours. When there is almost one in the world to proclaim His Name, existence will be meaningless. In the words of the Prophet, upon him be the best of blessings, the total destruction of the universe will take place when there exists almost no one who proclaims God.

In whatever way it is done, recitation is the safest and soundest of the ways leading to God. Without it, it is difficult to reach God. What an inexhaustible source of support and (spiritual) provision it is that man remembers Him in his conscience and puts this remembrance into words with his tongue and other faculties.

Recitation signifies a journeying toward Him. When a man starts to mention Him or recites His Names with his tongue and through his feelings and in his heart as a chorus, he finds himself in a mysterious lift and reaches the realm where spirits fly. He beholds through the slightly opened doors of the heavens indescribable scenes.

There is not a specific time for recitation of God's Names. Although the five, prescribed daily prayers which are the chief act or kind of worship and the mat of the vessel of the religion, are performed at five appointed times and cannot be done at certain times–during sunrise and sunset and when the sun is at zenith at noon–a man can mention God and recite His Names whenever He wishes. As declared in the verse, They mention God standing, sitting, and lying down (3.191), there is no restriction on recitation of God's Names with respect to either its time or the way of its performance.

It is difficult to encounter in the Qur'an and Sunna and the books of the righteous scholars who lived in the early centuries of Islam anything more strongly commended than recitation of God's Names. From daily prayers to holy struggle in the way of God, it is like the soul or blood of all kinds of worship.

The profundity or depth of a man's recitation is proportional to how deeply he feels God. This is what the Sufis call peace of heart or witnessing. Some mention God Almighty and reach Him in their hearts by a mysterious way. Some others know Him by their conscience and feel His constant Company by means of the point of reliance and the point of seeking help in their inner worlds. Since they uninterruptedly remember Him and mention Him by heart and conscience, since they always feel Him in their being and live fully aware of His ever presence, they come to regard mentioning Him (verbally) as heedlessness and ignorance of Him. A man of this degree of Dhikr says : 'God knows that I do not remember Him to mention Him just now. How should I remember and mention Him now, seeing that I have never forgotten Him.'

Tawba (Repetance)

Repetance (Tawba) simply means that one feels regret and is filled with remorse for wrongdoing and turns to God again with a new intention to make up what one has neglected. According to truth-seeking scholars, repentance signifies a sincere effort to be saved from opposing the Divine Essence in feelings, thoughts, intentions and acts and to sincerely comply with His commands and prohibitions. Repentance does not consist in feeling disgust at something bad or prohibited and giving up doing it. Repentance is remaining aloof from whatever God hates and prohibits, even life it seems agreeable to sense and reason.

Repentance is usually used together with 'nasuh', literally meaning pure, sincere, reforming, improving and repairing. Tawba nasuh-sincere and reforming repentance–means a pure, sincere repentance that perfectly reforms and improves. It is that one feels sincere, heart-felt and true remorse for the wrongdoing one commits and sets a good example for others in this respect. The Qur'an points to it where it mentions true repentance : O you who believe! Turn to God in true, sincere repentance. (66.8)

There are three categories of repentance :

(*a*) The first is the repentance of ordinary people who are unable to discern Divine truths. A man feels his disobedience to God as disquietude and, conscious of his sinfulness which clouds his heart, turns toward God and expresses his repentance with relevant words such as : 'I have fallen or committed a sin, forgive me'! Or, 'I ask for God's forgiveness.'

(*b*) Those half awakened to Divine truths beyond veils of material existence feel an inward thrill of sinfulness and remorse just after anything occurring to their minds or hearts incompatible with the consciousness of always being in the omnipresence of God or after every instance of heedlessness enveloping their hearts–they then immediately take refuge with the Mercy and Favour of God. One with such degree of wakefulness and spiritual alertness is as described in the following Tradition :

God's Messenger, upon him be peace and blessings, declared:

One who sincerely repents of his sin is as if he had never committed it. When God loves a servant of His, his sins do not harm him. Then he recited the verse : 'Assuredly, God loves the oft–repentant and those who always seek to purify themselves.'

When asked about the sign of repentance, he declared : It is heart-felt remorse.

(*c*) Those who live so careful a life that, as is declared in a tradition, even while they themselves are sleeping, their hearts are awake, immediately discard whatever intervenses between God and their hearts and other innermost faculties and regain the consciousness of their relation to the Light of the Lights. They always manifest the meaning of How excellent a servant! Truly he was ever turning in contrition (to his Lord). (38.44)

Repentance means regaining one's essential purity after every spiritual deformation, and frequent self-renewal [The stages of] repetance are :

1. One feels sincere, remorse and regret.

2. One frightens whenever one remembers other sins one has committed in the past.
3. One tries to eradicate injustice and support justice and right.
4. One reviews one's responsibilities and performs or makes up obligations neglected in the past.
5. One reforms oneself by removing spiritual defects caused by deviations and errors.
6. One regards and laments the times one has spent without mentioning or remembering God and thanking him and reflecting on his creation and is always apprehensive and alert that one's thoughts and feelings may be tainted by things that intervene between oneself and God. This last quality is characteristic of those who are greatly distinguished and are near to god.

If a man does not feel remorse, regret and disgust for the error he has committed, however great or small it is, and if he is not fearful and apprehensive that he may fall back into it at any time, and if he does not take shelter in servanthood to God and sincerity in servanthood in order to be freed from the deviations and errors into which he has lapsed as a result of falling away from God, his repetance will be no more than lying.

Mawlana Jalal al-Din Rumi says about sincere repetance :

I have repeated and turned to God so sincerely that I will not break [the vow of penitence] until my soul leaves my body. In fact, who other than an ass steps toward perdition after having suffered so much trouble on account of his sins?

Repentance is an oath of virtue, and holding steadfastly to it is heroism requiring a strong will-power. The lord of the penitents, upon him be peace and blessings, says that one who repents sincerely and holds steadfastly to it is of the rank of the martyrs, while the repentance of those who cannot be freed from their sins and deviations although they repeatedly repent of them means mocking the 'door' toward which the truly repentant ones turn in utmost sincerity and resolution.

A man who does not refrain from sins although he claims that he fears Hell, and does not do righteous deeds although he claims that he looks forward to Paradise, and is indifferent to the way and practices of the Prophet ﷺ (upon him be peace and blessings) although he asserts that he loves the Prophet, cannot be serious and true in his claims. So also it is difficult to accept as sincere and pure-hearted one who spends his life between turns of sins and shows of repentance.

The first station of an initiate is repentance, while the second is 'inaba' (sincere penitence). In everyday usage, 'inaba' is also used to express the ceremony held when a man submits himself to a spiritual guide (as a murshid). While repentance requires training feelings, thoughts and acts to direct them from opposition to admission and obedience, sincere penitence demands critique of the authenticity, sincerity and sufficiency of that admission and obedience. Repentance is a progressing or journeying toward God–meaning efforts to do whatever is pleasing to God and refraining from whatever is forbidden by Him. Sincere patience is an ascension through the stations of journeying in God meaning efforts to live an upright life in self annihilation and in absorption to seek God's good pleasure in whatever one does and thinks. Tawba (turning to God in contrition), is an ascension through the stations of journeying from God–meaning being responsible for guiding others after having embodied the islamic ways of belief, thought and conduct. In other words, taking refuge with God in fear of dying an unbeliever and deserving eternal punishment is repentance one's annihilating one's self in God with the desire of preserving one's spiritual rank is sincere penitence, and a man's closing himself to any other desires, ambitions or aims other than God's good pleasure is turning to God is utmost contrition. The first is the state of all believers and expressed in the verse; Repent you all to God, O believers! (24.31); the second is an attribute of saints and the foremost in belief and good conduct brought near unto God. Its beginning is to be seen in the verse, Turn to your Lord repentant (393.54) and its end is stated in, He comes with a contrite heart (50.33). The third is particular to Prophets and Messengers. God appreciates and praises them : How excellent a servant! Truly he was ever turning in contrition (to his Lord). (38.44)

The words expressing repentance uttered by those who are always conscious of being in the omnipresence of God in fact express sincere penitence or turning to God in contrition. It is in this sense that the words of the best of creation, upon him be peace and blessings, should be understood when he said : I ask God's forgiveness seventy or a hundred times a day. Repentance is the act or manner of those who try to live an upright life but rate unconscious of God's constant supervision of His servants and what nearness to God really means. Those who live in awareness of nearness to God regard it as heedlessness to turn to God in the way ordinary people do so, for He directs them whoever He wishes and constantly supervises them and is nearer to them than anything else. Their station is not the station of the people of the Unity of Being., ecstatic saints who view the creation completely annihilated in God and therefore accept God as the only truly existent being. It is the station of the people of the Unity of the Witnessed, the scholarly saints who accept that the truly existent one is He Who is witnessed or discerned beyond the creation. More than of those, it is the station of those progressing in the shadow of the practice of the Prophet Ahmad (Muhammad) ﷺ (upon him be peace and blessings) or in the light of the lamp of Muhammad. It is merely an assertion and groundless claim when those who are not of this station and live on [merely] the outer surface of other existence talk of Awba and inaba and especially of the final points of these two stations.

From the above we have seen that the Tasawwuf is Islamic mysticism which is commonly known as Sufism has its roots in the Quran itself and the tradition of other Prophet Mohammed and the Shahabas are also the earlier source of Sufism. However puritanic Islam as is being propagated now in the form of Tabligh does not recognise Sufism as Islamic. This is purely due to their gross misunderstanding or gross negligence or due to their intolerance of the fact that Sufism had imbibed and interwoven the ideas from Hinduism. The Holy Quran is full of mystical verses that are similar to the Vedic and Upanishadic mantras. The concept of Tawhid *i.e.*, the unity of the self with the supreme self is found scattered in the holy Quran. Reflecting upon God the Holy Quran says :

> *"God is the light of the heaven and earth. The likeness of this light is as a niche, in which there is a lamp. The lamp in a glass the glass as though it were a shining star-is kindled from a blessed tree, an olive that is neither of the west nor of the east, the oil of which nearly lights up without fire touching it. It is light upon light. God guides by his light those whom he wishes. God speaks to humanity in similitudes; God knows with all things."*[16]

The throne verse is equally mystical and speaks volumes about the God :

> *"God there is no God but him, the living the eternal, slumber does not affect hi, nor sleep. To him belongs the heaven and the earth. He knows what lies before them and behind them. His throne extends to the heaven and to the earth."*[17]

Thus Tasawwuf is Islamic mysticism which is the batin (esoteric) science of mysticism that leads one to realize the Supreme Reality.

References

1. Kashaf-al mahjub-Hujwiri.
2. Ibrahim Haqqi of Erzurum.
3. Ishavashyopanishad.
4. *Ibid.*
5. Ibrahim Haqqi Prophetic Tradition.
6. Quran 3.8.
7. Mathnavi y Rumi Translated by R.A. Nicholson.
8. Sahih Bukhari.
9. Quran 25.63.
10. *Ibid.,* 5.54.
11. *Ibid.,* 48.29.
12. *Ibid.,* 48.29.
13. Quran, 35.20.
14. Quran, 2.152.
15. Quran, 2.153.
16. Quran, 24.35 The light.
17. Quran Thorone verse 2.255.

Note : All references are from the Holy Quran unless otherwise mentioned.

Chapter 4
Manifest and Non-Manifest World

The question of the manifest and the non-manifest world has occupied a key position in Indian as well as western thoughts. Whether the phenomenal world that we experience exist. Whether there exist anything like Brahman or whether our life on earth is in existence in reality or it is merely a state of dream. If the Brahman is real and everything else is unreal what is to be said of the phenomenal world we see and experience. Is our sense experience real or merely elusive? All these and like questions have baffled the minds of the people but Philosophers, Seers and the Mystics have tried to answer them. The Upanishads unequivocally declare and establishe the supremacy of the Brahman or the Self. The great Indian Seer Shankara sees only Brahman as satya (real) everything else is illusory. Shankara's philosophy must be understood in relation to Brahman. Shankara never denies the existent world of sense perception but he stress that in relation to the Ultimate Reality the world is elusive. When one realizes the Ultimate Truth or the Ultimate Reality the sensory world becomes for him nothing but asat or false. When one sees Shankara says the rope in the dark, one takes it to be a snake but when one knows that it is because of the dark the rope was taken as a snake ethe false knowledge is removed and taken over by the Truth. In this way when the veil of Maya or avidya is removed the material world of phenomena does not hold water for the realized seer. When the Self or the brahman is realized there remains nothing to be realized. Now let us see what major Upanishads say about the manifestation and non-manifestation of the Ultimate Reality and the world of phenomena.

The Brihadaranyaka Upanishad talks about two forms of Reality :

"Verily there are two forms of Brahman, the formless and the formed, the mortal and the immortal, the moving and the unmoving, and the manifest and the unmanifest."

The Atma Upanishad very vividly and beautifully depicts the manifestation of the Supreme Reality. The following verses make it clear.

1. PURUSHA (highest Spirit) manifests itself in three modes :

As outer, inner, and supreme Self.
Skin, flesh, vertebral column, hair, fingers.
Toes, nails, ankles, stomach, navel, hips, thighs,
Cheeks, eyebrows, forehead, head, eyes, outer self.
The body, subject to birth and death[1].

This beautiful verse describes in detail not only the unmanifest nature of the Self but describes very specifically the essential evolution process. How the moral body develops and what are its different stages. The mystical nature of the Upanishads is seen here in this verse in its totality, magnanimity and beauty.

2. The inner self perceives the outside world.
Made up of earth, water, fire, air and space (akasha).
It is the victim of likes and dislikes,
Pleasure and pain, and delusion and doubt.
It knows all the subtleties of language,
Enjoys dance, music, and all the fine arts;
Delights in the senses, recalls the past,
Reads the Scriptures, and is able to act.
This is the mind, the inner person.

The second verse above is also beyond comparison. What the self can do when it takes the form of body or rather it enters the body. It can enjoy material things and need to read scriptures and follow the religious rituals prescribed by the cannons.[2]

3. The supreme Self, adored in the Scriptures,
Can be realized through the path of yoga.

Subtler than the banyan seed, subtler
than the hundred thousandth part of a hair,
This Self cannot be grasped, cannot be seen.
The supreme Self is neither born nor dies.
He cannot be burned, moved, pierced, cut, not dried.
Beyond all attributes, the supreme Self
is the eternal witness (shanta atman), ever pure,
Indivisible, and uncompounded,
Far beyond the senses and the ego.
In him conflicts and expectations cease.
He is omnipresent, beyond all thought,
without action in the eternal world.
Detached from the outer and the inner,
this supreme Self purifies the impure.
Om shanti shanti shanti[3]

In this verse or mantra the undestructiveness of the Self is described. The Self is indestructible, beyond the time and space, and is eternal and beyond the grasp and can be realized only through Yoga is described very minutely and beautifully. Upanishads herald that the phenomenal world has evolved out of the Brahman and it is the spontaneous evolution.

"He was alone and He desired let me multiply" and lo...the world evolved out of Him. Let us see what different Upanishads have to say about the evolution of the world.

Unpanishads describes the four aspects of Brahaman. They are :

1. Non-Being
2. Iswara
3. Hiranya Garbha and
4. Viraj

1. Non-Being

The pure Non-Being or the unmanifest is the First principle. Variously described as the Ancient and the one without a beginning and without an end and the one without a second, very little indeed is known about this Eternal, imperishable, and the unchangeable principle. The Upanishadic seers were content with such description as "This", "That" or "It" when they spoke of this Eternal Principle, trying to make it comprehensible to the evolving minds of their disciples.

We are told that it is beyond all. There the mind does not go, nor the senses, nor our understanding. It is always in front of the senses and intelligence. It is only through personal experience perhaps one may grasp a little about it. But even about this we are not sure.

It is doubtful whether any one can really experience something which does not exist or which is simply non-existence or non-Being and come back to us and describe it to us in the normal planes of thought. "Non-existent does one become if a person knows Brahman as Non-Being." (Taittiriya Upanishad 11.6.1).

The evolution of the world is very beautifully described in the Taitiriya Upanishad in the following words :

"From Brahman came space, from space air,
From air fire, from fire water, from water
Earth; from earth, plants; from plants, food;
And from food,
The human body, head, arms, legs and heart."[4]

The following verses from the Aitareya Upanishad also very vividly describe the spontaneous creation of the world :

"Atma va idam eka evagra asit, naanyat kin cana misat sa
Aikasta lokan nu sruja iti."

(before the world was created, the self-Alone existed; nothing whatever stirred. Then the self thought : "Let me create the world")

"sa imamal lokan asrjata, ambho marichir maram apombhah
parena divam; dyayuh, pratishtha, antariksham marichayah,

prithvi maro ya adhastat ta apah."

(He brought forth all the worlds out of him self : Ambhas, high above the sky; Marichi, the sky; Mara, the middle region that is earth; And Apa, the realm of waters below.)

"sa iksta ime nu loka, loka palan nu sruja iti;
So' dhbhya eva purusam samudhrtyamurchayat."

(The self thought : "I have created these worlds. Let me now create guardians for these worlds." From the waters he drew forth Purusha.)

"And give him a form. As the self brooded Over the form, a mouth opened, as does an egg, giving forth speech and fire; nostrils opened with the power of breathing the air; eyes opened, giving rise to sight and sun; And ears opened to hear the sound in space. Skin appeared and from it hair; from hair came plants and trees. The heart gushed forth; from the heart came the mind, and from the mind came the moon. The navel opened with the downward force, Apana, which gave rise to death. The sex organ rose with living water which gave rise to birth."

Everything is created out of the Brahman. The Brahman is the first cause of creation.

The problem is that the human mind which is accustomed to the language of the words and symbols cannot grasp the Absolute Truth that cannot really be compared to anything else. Even the devas and the gods of still higher planes have little understanding of it, is evident from the descriptive accounts of gods encounter with it in the kena Upanishad.

We do not even know why in the first place. He created all this. The explanation that He created these worlds and beings for His delight or Ananda is too simplistic an explanation to satisfy the inquisitive curiosity of a well developed mind. If the Absolute creates something out of something else, be it a cause, a purpose or some reason, then that cause, purpose or reason, would be above Him and He cannot be called the Absolute.

If the Absolute is eternal and timeless and is not subject to any causative principle or the dimensions of time and space, how could there be any gap between Him and His creation? He and His creation must have happened simultaneously, without a second, without any distinction or differentiation.

Surely the creative process must have begun without any reason, without any motive, almost as if it was a spontaneous process, without the intervention of Time and space or a process at the Absolute level.

That the process of creation is spontaneous and without a cause would perhaps rattle many religious minds, but we have no better explanation to offer than this if we want to accept the First principle of the universe as the Absolute, Eternal, Infinite and eternal Truth.

Perhaps there was a beginning to the process of creation but it might never come to a permanent conclusion as the Creative Principle that manifested out of Him is also eternal and beyond dissolution as we understand in the subsequent paragraphs.

2. Iswara

When God wakes up from His sleep He becomes Iswara! In His awakened state He exercises His creative will and sets in motion the creative process. Thus Iswara is the creative Spirit, the Being, the awakened Non-Being, the Saguna Brahman, the brahman with qualities, who exercising His will, His Power and His wisdom creates the worlds and the world order (Rita)

He is the Truth Consciousness, the combination and knowledge and will, the directing and causative aspect of the Universal Self. He is the creative consciousness, who in the aspect of Purusha (the Universal Male) joins with His other aspect Prakriti (Divine Energy) and brings forth the worlds and the beings. The word "Brah" means 'to grow or to burst forth'. Thus Iswara is the Brahman who bursts out of his own sleep (non existence).

As the creator, sustainer and destroyer of the worlds, He is also the Trinity, Brahma, Vishnu and Mahesha. They are but one though they appear differently to the mortal world. They are the three qualities of His Primal Nature (Prakriti), and the three aspects of his Will and consciousness (Purusha), in their pure and primordial states, which wake up as He wakes up and regulate the creation.

In the Maitri Upanishad we are given an account of the conception of the trinity, how darkness (tamas) represented by Siva, passion (rajas) represented by Brahma and goodness (sattva) represented by Vishnu got differentiated from the Highest. (Maitri Upanishad V.2)

While we have no idea of what the Non-Being or the Nirakar Brahman truly is, we have the accounts of the Upanishadic seers who through self contemplation realized Iswara and described Him as Sat chit Ananda, Truth, Consciousness and Bliss. This experience becomes possible in human beings because in the individual being, Iswara is verily Atman.

In the Katha Upanishad says Lord Yama to the young Nachiketa," By knowing through self-contemplation (adhyatma yoga) that Primal Being who is difficult to be seen, who is very mysterious, who is hidden in the cave (of ones heart) and who is situated deep (within one self), the wise men (dhira) leave behind both joy and sorrow.

It must be noted that there is no real distinction between Saguna Brahman and Nirguna Brahman. They are the different states of the Parameswara the one only Eternal Principle. When the Non-Being awakens He becomes Iswara and when Iswara takes rest at the end of creation He becomes non-Being. This seems as if the Reality plays hide and seek with the seers. This hide and seek becomes the mystic experience for the seers.

3. Hiranya Garbha

He is the World Soul (Mahan Atma), the Cosmic Egg, that arises out of cosmic waters and engages Himself in the creation of forms and beings. He is the First Born (prathamja), who manifests forms that are already contained in Him.

He is the Sutratman (the soul of a necklace) the thread on which all beings and all the worlds (the world of the devas, of the ancestors, of the humans, of the demons etc.) are strung like beads in a necklace.

While Iswara is the causative principle (karanabhutam),

Hiranyagarbha is the dynamic or the active principle (kriyabhutam or karyabhutam). He is also called Brahma who as the creative and dynamic principles uses the forms existing in Him and brings forth the Beings.

The word "brah" means "bursting out or bringing forth" and "ahm" means ego. Brahma is therefore one who brings forth many "ahms" or egos or beings not this world using his divine power and matter and pouring life (breath) into them. Hiranyagarbha is not an eternal being, but comes into existence at the beginning of creation and becomes dissolved in Iswara at the end of creation.

4. Viraj

Viraj is the manifest world, that which is created, or which is brought forth. He is the result of the creative process set in motion by Iswara and accomplished by Hiranyagarbha. He is the manifested aspect of Iswara through the hands of the latter.

It is a world that is in perpetual motion and subject to illusion. It is a reality that is different and distinct in nature from that of Iswara or Hiranyagarbha since the interplay of the guns (qualities), the elements and the senses result in the formation of numerous individual beings and ego forms (ahamkaras) who suffer from the illusion of individuality and feelings of separateness. Viraj like Hiranyagarbha is also subject to dissolution at the end of creation.

Thus the mystical experiences of everything evolving spontaneously out of the brahman or the Self is the unique concept of the Upanishads. The manyness disappears when the Chandogya Unpanishad proclaims as "that thou art"

The Islamic concept of Manifest and non-manifest world :

Islamic oral traditions say that the world is created out of Nur of Ilahi that is out of the light or the spirit of Allah. This concept of creation of the world seems very akin to the concept of Hiranyagarbha of Indian mysticism. In the beginning there was none only vacuum reigned everywhere. God desired to create the world and he created the world out of his Supreme Ruh (spirit). Let us see what recorded literature says about the evolution of the world. The religious edifice of Islam is based upon the foundation stone of Tawhid (The unity of Allah) and therefore the religion of Islam does advocate unitariness of Allah but the unitariness of Allah is not like the upanishadic unity of Self with the Supreme Reality. Islam does not recognise the unity of the soul nafs with that of the Ruh Spirit. It also does not recognise the absolute Unity like Shankara's Advaita but the concept is that of absolute monotheism.

The Persian Sufi Mehmud Shabistri in his Gulshane Raaz (The Rose Garden of Divine Mystery) sings of the Islamic Spirituality in the following lines;

> *"See the one utter the one, know the one,*
> *For this is the seal of the root and branches of faith."*

Seyyed Hossein Nasr in his monumental compilation of Islamic Spirituality says : Islamic spirituality is the seeing of the One, uttering the name of the one, and knowing the one who is God in his absolute Reality beyond all manifestations and determinations, the One to whom the Quran refers as Allah. The whole of Islam is based on the doctrine of Tawhid that is the Unity of Being. But what can specifically be called the Islamic spirituality is the experience and knowledge of the Unity and its realization in thoughts, words, acts and deeds through the will, the soul and intelligence. This spirituality is ultimately to live and act according to the will of God and accordingly love him with one's whole being, and finally to know him through that knowledge which integrates and illuminates and whose realization is never divorced from love nor possible without correct action.

The Manifestation of the Divine

Since words are but manifestations of objects, concepts, and truths, the Sufi feels that by continuous and complete attention to the meaning and reality of his remembrance of God and by constant contemplation (Dhikra) he becomes the true manifestation of that remembrance. That is to say, with continuous, selfless remembrance a Divine Attribute comes to predominate in the being of the Sufi.

The Sufis consider that there is a particular Divine Attribute, which dominates the being of every prophet and saint, such that they can be said to be the incarnation of that attribute. For example, Sufis feel that Moses is the manifestation of the transcendent aspect of Reality, because of his ability to speak with God without a mediator. In the Qur'an, the lord said to Moses, "Do not fear, because you are transcendent." Jesus is the manifestation of prophethood. While an infant he cried, "God gave me the book and placed me as a prophet."

All the prophets are manifestations of the Divine Unity and Perfection, but according to the Islamic notion Mohammed ﷺ is its supreme manifestation. His name is the most exalted of the Divine Names, containing all the Names within it. Thus, Mohammed ﷺ is the spiritual incarnation and manifestation of all of God's Names. Mohammed ﷺ himself said, "What God first created was my Light." Out of this light and for this light the manifest world is created.

In addition, each prophet is the manifestation of one of the Divine Attributes, and all of the Attributes are contained in the most exalted Name. Also, Mohammed is the manifestation of the Great Name. So, due to the fact that his manifestation is inclusive of all the Names, he hierarchically comes before all other created things, and for the same reason said, "I was a prophet while Adam was still between water and earth."

Here we find the basic difference between the Upanishadic and the Islamic concept of manifestation. Upanishads state that the Self is Brahman and out of this self everything evolved. The self and the Brahman are not separate but only because of false knowledge that is Maya one differentiates as the two. This is known as Advaita or absolute Reality. The great Indian Mystic Saint Shankaracharya has propounded the theory of Maya to establish the supremacy of Brahman. Shankaracharya says that only Brahman is true. Everything except the Brahman is false (Brahman satyam jagat mithya). It is only because of Avidya or maya (false knowledge) that we take things as they appear to us. He further establishes the unity of the Self with the jiva (jivo brahmaiv naparaha). Here Shankara's idea is not to deny the wordly objects as we encounter in our daily life. Shankaracharya wants to drive home the idea that when Brahmanis realized everything, every object of manifest world becomes false. The theory of Maya must be understood in relation to Brahman and only then the dictum SARVAM KHALU IDAM BRAHMAN (everything is full of Brahman) becomes true.

This charisma happens only to the seers, mystics and those who are on the path of Fana, Rumi in one of his mystical poems says :

"First he appeared in the realm inanimate;
Thence came into the world of plants and lived
The plant life many a year, nor called to mind
What he had been; then took the onward way
To animal existence, and once more
Remembers naught of what life vegetative,
Save when he feels himself moved with desire
Towards it in the season of sweet flowers,
as babes that seek the breast and know not why.
Again the wise Creator whom thou knowest
Uplifted him from animality
To Man's estate; and so from realm to realm
Advancing, he became intelligent,
Cunning and keen of wit, as he is now.
No memory of his past abides with him;
And from his present soul he shall be changes.
Though he is fallen sleep, God will not leave him
in this forgetfulness. Awakened, he
Will laugh to think what troubled dreams he had.
And wonder how his happy state of being
He could forget, and not perceive that all
Those pains and sorrows were the effect of sleep
And guile and vain illusion. So this world
Seems lasting, though 'tis but the sleepers' dreams;
Who, when the appointed Day shall dawn, escapes
From dark imaginings that haunted him,
And turns with laughter on his phantom griefs
When he beholds his everlasting home.[5]"

The great Sufi mystic and peer ShaikhAbdul Qadir Jilani in his The Secrets of the Secret says in the following words regarding the manifestation of the ultimate Reality and the evolution of the world.

> *"Allah most high first created, from the divine light of his own beauty the light of Mohammed*ﷺ*. He declares this in a divine tradition related from Him by the Prophet*ﷺ*.*

I have created the soul of Mohammed ﷺ from the light of my Manifestation (Wajh).

This is declared by our master the messenger of Allah in his words : "Allah first created my soul-created the divine light and the pen. He then created the intellect.' What all that is mentioned as having been created first mean is the creation of the truth of Mohammedﷺ, the hidden reality of Mohammedﷺ he is also [like his Lord] called by many beautiful names. He is called nur, the divine Light, because he was purified of the darkness hidden under the attribute of the might and wrath (Jalal) of Allah. Allah Most high says in his Holy Qur'an;

"There has come to you from Allah a light and perspicuous Book. (Sura Maida, 15)[6]. He is called the Total intellect (aql al–kull) because he saw and understood everything. He is called the pen (al-qalam) because he spread wisdom and knowledge, and he poured knowledge into the realm of letters."

The soul of Mohammed ﷺ is the essence of all beings, the beginning and the reality of the universe. He indicates this with the words, I am from Allah and the believers are from me. Allah most high created all souls from his soul is the realm of the first created beings, in the best of forms. 'Mohammed' is the name of all humanity in the realm of souls ('alam al-arwah'). He is the source of the home of each and everything.

Four thousand years after the creation of the light of the Mohammedﷺ, Allah created the Heavenly Throne (arsh) from the light of the eye of Mohammed. He created the rest of the creation from the Heavenly throne. Then he sent the soul to descend to the lowest levels of creation, to the realm of this material world, to the realm of matter and bodies. Then we make him descend to the lowest of the low ('Sura Tin, 5). He sent that light from where it was created, from the Ultimate realm ('alam al-lahut) which is the realm of the manifestation of the Allah's Essence, of unity, of absolute being-to the realm of the divine Names, the manifestation of the divine attributes, the dressed the souls in the robs of light. These souls are called 'Sultan Souls'. Cloth in the light they descended to the realm of the angles. There he clothed them with the brilliant robes of the angels; there they were called 'spiritual souls'. Then he caused them to descend to the world of matter, of water and fire, earth and ether they became human souls. Then from this world he created the bodies of flesh. "From it we created you and into it we shall return you, and from it raise a second time ('Sura Ta Ha'55)."[7]

After this stage, Allah ordered the souls to enter into their bodies, and by His will they entered. So when I have made him complete and breathed into him of my soul...('Sura Sad, 72).

A time came when these souls started binding themselves to the flesh and forgot their source and their covenant. They forgot that when Allah created them in the realm of the souls he had asked them Am I Not Your Lord..? And they had answered indeed they forgot their promise they forgot their source their way to return home but Allah is merciful the source of all help and security for his creation. He had mercy upon them so he sent divine books and messengers to them to remind them of their origin. The holy Quran reveals that :

And certainly we sent Moses with our messages. Bring forth the people from darkness into light and remind them of the days of Allah. ('Sura Ibrahim'5).

Many messengers have come to this world fulfilled their duties and passed away. The purpose of all was to bring man the message and awaken people to heedfulness. But people who remembered him, who turned towards him, people who wished to return to their divine origin fewer and fewer with the passage of time.

The prophets continued coming and the divine message continued until there appeared the great spirit of Mohammed the last of the messengers who saved people from destruction. Allah most high sent him to open the eyes of the heats of the heedless. His purpose to awaken them from the sleep of unconsciousness and to unite them with the eternal beauty, with the cause with, the essence of Allah. Allah further says in the Holy Qur'an :

Say : this is my way I called to Allah with the certainty of insight-I and those who follow me.[8] ('Sura Yusuf' 108).

The messenger of Allah says, my companion are like the star in the sky. Which ever you them follow you will find the true path. This insight comes from the eye of the soul. This insight opens the eye in the hearts of those who are close to Allah. This is the message of the Prophet, which is full of mystical allusions and is shrouded in the pages of Holy Qura'n and in the teachings of the Sufis. The creation of the world is described in many Suras of the Quran. Let us see one of them. The Quran says :

"KHALAQA -KUM MIN NAFS WAAH. IDAH THUMMA JACALA MIN-HAAZAWJ-HA WAANZALALA–KUM MIN AL-ANCAAM THAMAANIYAH AZWAAJ YAKHLUQ-KUM FE BUT.ON 'UMMAHAAT -KUM KHALQ (AN) MIN BACDI KHALQ FE Z.ULUMAAT THALAATH DHAALIKUM ' ALLAAH RABB-KUMLA–HU AL-MULKLAA 'ILAAH' ILLAA HUWA FA-' ANNAA TUS.RAFON"[9]

He created you (all) from a single person : then created of like nature his mate; and He sent down for you eight head of cattle in pairs : He makes you in the wombs of your mothers in stages one after another in three veils of darkness. Such is Allah your Lord and Cherisher : to Him belongs (all) dominion. There is no God but He : then how are ye turned away?[10] (from your true Centre) The goal of Islam is to lead the people to the right path to save them from the evil and evildoers. The people of the book as the Quran says must save themselves from the perverted path and follow the way the Prophet has shown to them and Allah has revealed through Gabriel via Prophet Mohammed to the people. The opening verse of the Quran Al-Fatiha is very clear and self-explanatory. It is the preamble of the Quran and it reveals in beautiful words the goal for mankind. It is the prayer mantra of the Quran in which one seeks from God the blessings and asks for the right path. The prayer mantra is known as Al-Fatih which seems to me very similar to Upanishadic prayer mantras is the declarative Sura of the Quran in which is sought the right way and the right path. The path of those prophets and the people on whom the mercy, clemency and kindness of Allah was bestowed. The AL Fatiha is the face of the holy Quran as Sura Yasin is the heart of the Quran.

References

1. Atma Upanishad.
2. *Ibid.*
3. Atma Upanishad Verse 2.
4. *Taitiriya Upanishad II 1.1.*
5. R.A. Nicholsin *'Persian Poems'*, an Anthology of verse translations edited by A.J. Arberry, Everyman's Library, 1972.
6. The Quran.
7. The Quran.
8. *Sura Yusuf' 108.*
9. The Quran.
10. Sura 39, VI.

Chapter 5

The Meaning of Life and the Concept of Salvation

In Greek mythology, there is story of Sisyphus that is well known as the myth of Sisyphus. In this story, Sisyphus is assigned a task of rolling the log up on a high hill and then throwing it rolling down and further rolling it up and down again and again without any pause. Such monotonous and laborious task imposed upon him as a penalty becomes the starting point to find out the meaning of life for the western thinkers. The western scholars have tried to weave a philosophy of the meaning of life from this story. As per this story and the subsequent philosophy developed out of it known as existentialism examines the question of meaning of life. Accordingly, the theory states that there is no aim of and no meaning of life. Life is nothing but the incessant activity imposed upon man by almighty God. This philosophy also examines the question of free will and human liberty, which is not my purpose here to discuss in detail. The literary movement developed out of this existentialist point of view is known as theory of absurdity. The Indian philosophy and Sufism is quite different. The oriental philosophy of life is quite in contrast to the occidental view of life.

The Upanishads and Sufism have a positive view about life. Life according to Upanishads is not meaningless full of sound and fury signifying nothing but life is full of meanings. God has not imposed upon human being life as a punishment but life is a divine gift given to humankind. The aim of life according to Upanishads is to realize self and after fulfilling the assigned task of realizing the self ultimately to merge with the Supreme Reality.

In the beginning, there was only Self and this self desired and then multiplied into many. The first stanza of the Isha

Upanishad says volumes about the meaning of life and the completeness of the Self that is *Brahman.*

"Om puranam adah purnam idam purnat purnam udachyte,
Purnasya purnamaddaya purnam evavashishgate.
Om shantih, shantih, shantih.

This mantra brings out the mystery of the universe through the cause and effect relationship. *Purnam adah purnam idam,* meaning : "That is complete, this is complete." The word adah (*That*) refers to the Supreme Reality, Paramatma (the cause) and the word Idam (this) refers to the entire animate and inanimate manifestation (the effect) pervaded by the Supreme Reality. The Supreme Reality is beyond this manifestation and is extremely greater. Further, **purnat purnam udacyat**, meaning : "From the complete (Paramatma), only the complete manifestation (this universe) has emanated, because incomplete cannot be the result of the complete. The doctrine is : "Whatever is there in the causal form, that itself transforms into the effect form. The effect of the complete cannot be incomplete." Continuing, the mantra declares : **"Purnasya purnam adaya purnam eva avashishyat",** meaning "From *that* complete when this complete is negated, is taken away, what remains is still complete." It might look absurd, but it can be understood by way of an example. When taking away zero from zero, the result is still zero. Similarly subtracting infinity from infinity, what remains is still infinity.

In this mantra, it has been declared that every living being is complete in itself as the Supreme Atman is. There may be difference in size and form, but in essence and quality there is no difference. The Shruti (Veda) also says Ayamatma brahma, Sohamasmi–This Atman is Brahma, I am that. Once it is realized that the Atman manifested in our form is complete Sat-Cid-Ananda, self-consciousness increases greatly. If there is still any doubt about our own completeness despite the declaration of the Vedas, then, inquire why this feeling is? But for this, one has to take recourse in Brahmavidya; surrender to a self realized preceptor master of this knowledge. After the benedictory mantra, in the first mantra of the Ishopanishad, an unparalleled message has been given for the mankind. In Brihadaranyaka Upanishad the sage Yajnavalkya wants to distribute his property between his two wives Maitreyi and Katyayani so he calls both of them and the discussion on immortality takes place. Maitryi asks Yajnavalkya that can she attain immortality if she possesses all the wordly wealth. In answer to this question the sage replies that she cannot get immortality what she can get with wealth is that she can live the life like the rich people with all wordly pleasures but she cannot attain immortality with the material wealth. The sage stresses the point that no one can buy immortality with money. The central theme of this Upanishad is concentration or contemplation or realization of the Self which is eternal, deathless beyond time and space. As per this Upanishad the love prevails not because of the object subject relationship but because of the self. The husband loves the wife and the wife loves husband, the children love parents and the parents love the children, the gods are loved and the wealth is loved or everything is loved not because of that thing but because the Self lives in those things. Hence the Self must be realized by meditation or contemplation on it. If one realizes the Self nothing is left to realize or for understanding. Those who mistakes and separates them as different from the Self the confusion arises.

There is no dispute regarding the self-realization as the motive or the goal according to the Upanishadic Philosophy. Still however there are four Purusharthas which are of the utmost importance according to the Hindu Philosophy. These four purusharthas are Dharma, Artha, Kama and Moksha. They are called the great Purusharthas or the goals or the ends in life. The Purusharthas :

Dharma

Dharma means righteousness and good moral and ethical practices in accordance with the scriptures. Dharma includes all duties–personal, social and religious. Dharma is considered as the first of the four human goals, because it is the most comprehensive and is valid through out the life. The word "Dharma" is derived from the root "dhr" meàns the principle which upholds, supports and nourishes the life of human beings. It is the supporting principle of the universe. The word Religion in English language is not enough to express the meaning and significance of the word Dharma. This word Dharma implies not only a religious and philosophical framework, but a total worldview, including a moral order, right conduct. It is the universal law of nature that upholds the cosmos. According to Bhagwad-Gita and Smritis 'Dharma' means, the privileges, duties and obligations of a man, his standard of conduct as member of the Aryan community, as a member of one of the classes as a person in a particular stage of life. Dharma consists of many characteristics, such as Ahimsa-non violence, Satya-Truthfulness, Asteya-non-stealing, Saucha-purity of conduct, Indri-yanigraha-control of senses, Dhih-wisdom, Vidya-learning or knowledge, Akrodha-non-anger, etc. Dharma or righteous path followed, sincerely, brings success and fame in this life and unparalleled happiness in the life here after.

Artha : (Possessions or Material Wealth)

Artha means Wealth or Material prosperity is the second pursuit of human life. It is very important goal on which social activities and material pleasure depends. Purity of means is emphasized by the Hindu lawmakers, while earning the wealth. Wealth is a kind of power, which affects human mind and behaviour. Acquisition of money with ignoble means is prohibited.

Artha is not an end in itself but it is a basic necessity, one must earn enough wealth in order to raise a family and maintain a household. This is an earthly or material wealth. The Spiritual wealth is to attain self-realization.

Wealth must not be for hoarding but for sharing with those who are poor, handicapped or less fortunate.

Dharma and Artha must be coordinated in order to earn decent living; Artha is not an ultimate end of Hindu religious life.

Kama

Kama indicates the needs and desires of body and mind in the form of requirements, passions, emotions and drives. Kama or the desire is the third goal of human life. It is fulfillment of desires. Renunciation or detachment to wordly desires is certainly not suited to the commoner. Only rare people can renounce all desires. Common man can enjoy sensual and other pleasures, but the enjoyment of desires should be on righteous path. Lord Krishna says in the Gita that, 'I am the Kama (desire, sex) which is not opposed to Dharma.' Sex is not considered sinful in Hinduism. Sex, not violatory of social order is permitted.

Hindu thinkers have recognized that without enjoyment of sensuous objects, complete understanding of life is not possible. Therefore, the concept of Kama is incorporated in the Hindu ethos.

In Hinduism there is a separate branch of science of sex. The science gives a technique of deriving maximum sensuous pleasures. For the gratification of sexual desire, one is required to get married and become a householder. Artha and Kama are goals, if they are not opposed to Dharma. Virtue consists in leading a life of duty, living in harmony and peace with developing of character and uplift of soul. Artha and Kama are necessary goals for the stability, interaction and development of society as well as life of individual. Righteous means are recommended to achieve these goals for the healthy development of the individual and the society. Satisfaction of genuine human desires such as art, music, pleasant food, sports, marital love, filial affections, clothes, jewellery etc. are not suppressed but must be satisfied in a controlled manner. Through controlled satisfaction of genuine desires and passions, an individual becomes free from Kama

Freedom from sensual desires and passion is necessary for attaining Moksha and is made possible by the proper harmonization of Dharma, Artha, and Kama.

Moksha : (Moksha means freedom from cycles of birth and death.) Its aim is to make an individual a better person, so that he/she can live harmoniously in this world and seek union with God. Moksha means liberation from wordly entanglements. This is the ultimate goal of human life. It is noteworthy, that the principle of duty for duty's sake is never accepted by the Hindu thinkers. Though these ideals seem to be lofty, it is barren and unattractive, because every one is keen to know why he is performing his duties. In Hinduism, ignorance is a cause of bondage and Dharma is the means of liberation. All other three Purusarthas are complementary to it. This concept of Moksha or liberation is peculiar to Indian religions.

Hinduism has probed deep into the mystery of human life and come to the conclusion that life is not jut the period between birth and death. The spirit are souls in human body is indestructible but it goes through various cycle of birth and death (Samsara). On account of ignorance and its own Karma (Action) the highest purpose of human life is to realize ones own nature and break way from recurrence of births and deaths. Death is not end of life. It is a beginning of new life. Just like one casts off worn out clothes and wears new one, similarly soul casts off its worn out body and enters new one to enjoy fruits of its own deeds, good or bad.

According to Hinduism Moksha means absolute cessation of suffering. Vedanta states that it is a state of supreme bliss. Liberation is the highest spiritual values for the Hindus.

Dharma, Artha, Kama and Moksha are the four Purusharthas that govern our activity. Dharma is the proper rules of one's duty, which literally means, "that which holds" the universe and its beings. They are classified as Samanya Dharma or the general and universal rules and Visesha Dharma or specific personal rules for each individual. They give peace, joy, strength and tranquility. Artha and Kama are the materialistic desire and passion that also govern our actions. Unless one seeks the material benefits and pleasures within the scope of Dharma, it will cause grief with greed and lust. Moksha is the relief from pain and suffering and ultimate liberation that is the main reason for all our actions and that is the aim or goal of individual soul.

Meaning and Goal of Life According to Islam

The Islamic concept of life is also like the Vedantic concept of life. Man was created for the realization of the Lord hence realizing the lord and finally to become one with the Supreme Reality is the aim of life according to Sufism. The concepts of Islamic mysticism Fana and Baqa are sufficient to explain to us the meaning of life. No doubt some Sufi cults do stress on saint veneration and worship of the God like Bhakti cult but the pure Sufistic way is that of God realization as it is propounded Brahman realization in the Upanishads. The concept of Fana and Baqa are as under in detail :

Fana

Fana means annihilation in the way of merging with the Supreme Reality. There are conflicts regarding the true nature of Fana, Sayeed Kharraj says that "annihilation is annihilation of consciousness of manhood (ubudiyyat), and subsistence is subsistence in the contemplation of Godhead. (Ilahiyyat)".

Hujwiri in his Kashful Mahjub explains this concept very elaborately. He says, "It is an imperfection to be conscious in one's action that one is a man and one attains real manhood." Fana is the disappearance of Aniyat (the I ness) of the traveller in the I ness of God. In Fana the essence attributes and the actions of the Shalik (the traveller) becomes the essence attributes and the actions of the God. This concept is accepted by all Indian Sufis.

There are three stages or degrees or stations in Fana. They are :

1. Qurbe-Farid (Nearness to obligation)
2. Qurbe-Nawafil (Nearness to superogation)
3. Jama-Baynul-Qurbayn (the Union of two nearness)

In the first stage the seer has no actions of his own, he becomes an instrument in the hands of God and he acts through him. In the second stage the order is reversed and the God becomes an instrument and acts according to the orders of the seeker. In the third stage the seer or the seeker or the mystic or the Sufi finds himself neither as an instrument nor as an agent but he merges with the essence of the Supreme Reality or the God.

Prof. R.A. Nicholson in this regards says that : "The enraptured Sufi who has passed beyond the illusion of subject and object and broken through to the oneness can neither deny that he is anything nor affirm that he is all things." These are the two negative and the positive aspect of cosmic consciousness. Mawlana Rumi has nicely illustrated these ideas of Fana in the following lines :

> *"O Muslims what can I do? For I do not know myself*
> *I am not a Christian nor a Jew nor a fire worshipper, nor a Muslim.*
> *I am not of the east or the West, nor of Land nor of Sea.*
> *I am neither of the elements nor of the circling Spheres*
> *I am neither of earth nor of air, of water or fire.*[1]"

The negative aspect in the above lines is very nicely depicted by Rumi. In the same way the positive aspect is portrayed in the following lines.

> *"O Mussulmans!*
> *Is there any lover in the world? Then I am He!*
> *Muslim, Pagan, Christian, Monk? Lo I am He!*
> *Shibli, Karkhi, Bayazid and Junayd,*
> *Bu-Hanifa, Shafi, Malik, I am He!*
> *Yes I am Injil, Psalter, Quran utterly*
> *O Shams–Tabriz, what is the end of your claim?*
> *Here Then The Gist : The soul of the soul I am He!*[2]"

The concepts of baqa also need explanation in detail. Baqa means the outer world, the manifest world. In terms of Sufism Baqa is the station of Shari'a. The clerics and the Kazis who interpret the Islamic laws remains on the stage of Baqa. The Umma (the people) lives according to the exoteric principles of the Shari'a, but Sufis cross the border of the Shari'a and reaches the stage of Fana. The Sufi recognizes the three great journeys. They are as under :

1. **Sayr ILA LLah :** (Journey towards Allah). In this journey the seeker embarks from the world of creation to the world of command or from the world of manifestation to the world of non-manifestation. The seeker has to cross the two stages of Wahididyat and Wahdat *i.e.,* Divine devolution. The journey of the Salik then ends into haqiqate-Muhammadi (the realization of Truth).

2. **Sayr Fi-allah :** (Journey into Allah) In this journey the Salik melts into the essence of God. This stage is called the stage of Adiyat. Hallaj Mansur when reached this stage cried out Anal-Haq in Divine ecstasy. His words were :

> *"I am He whom I love and He whom I love is I*
> *We are two spirits in one body*
> *If thou seest me thou seest Him*
> *And if thou seest Him thou seest us both"*[3]

3. **Sayr ani 'Ilah :** (Journey from God) This journey is a back journey from god. It is the journey from non-manifest to the manifest world. This stage is called Baqa and can be compared well with the mythic bird phoenix which burns itself and revives back or come to life from its burnt ashes. The Salik after already having been annihilated into God comes back to the world of manifestation. Such Saliks do bring with them the attributes of Supreme Reality. Talking about Fana and Baqa Hazrat Peer Inayat Khan a Sufi himself says :

> *"Belief in God is the first step. By the belief in God is attained the losing oneself in God. If one is able to do it, one has attained a power which is beyond human comprehension.*

The process of attaining this is called Fana by the Sufis. Fana is not necessarily destruction in God. Fana results in what may be called a resurrection in God, which is symbolized by the picture of Christ. The Christ on the cross is narrative of Fana; it means, 'I am not.' And the idea of resurrection explains the next stage, which is Baqa, and which means, 'Thou art', and this means rising towards All-might. The divine spirit is to be recognized in that rising towards All-might. Fana is not attained by torturing oneself, by tormenting oneself, by giving 'oneself a great many troubles, as many ascetics do. For even after torturing themselves, they will not come to that realization if they were not meant to. It is by denying one's little self, the false self which covers one's real self, in which the essence of divine Being is to be found.

Let us understand the true nature of this journey by raising doubts and putting questions :

What is this journey taken by the soul from the source to manifestation and from manifestation back to the same source which is the goal? Is it a journey, or is it not a journey? It is not a journey in truth. It is a change of experience which makes it a journey, a story; and yet a whole journey produced in moving pictures is in one film which does not journey for miles and miles, as it appears to do on the screen.

Do many journeys or one? Many while still in illusion; and one when the spirit has disillusioned itself. Who journeys, is it man or God? Both and yet one : the two ends of one line. What is the nature and character of this manifestation? It is an interesting dream. What is this illusion caused by? By cover upon cover; the soul is covered by a thousand veils. Do these covers gave happiness to the soul? Not happiness, but intoxication. The farther the soul is removed from its source, the greater the intoxication. Does this intoxication help the purpose of the soul's journey towards its accomplishment? It does in a way, but the purpose of the soul is accomplished by its longing. And what does it long for? Sobriety. And how is that sobriety attained? By throwing away the veils, which have covered the soul, and thus divided it from its real source and goal. What uncovers the soul from these veils of illusion? The change which is called death. This change can be forced upon the soul against its desire, and I then called death. This is a mot disagreeable experience like snatching away the bottle of wine from a drunken man, which is most painful to him for a time. Or the change can be brought about at will, and the soul throws away the cover that surrounds it and attains the same experience of sobriety while on earth, even if it is be but a glimpse of it. This is the same experience which the soul arrives at after millions and millions of years, drunk with illusion; and yet not exactly the same.

The experience of the former is Fana, annihilation, but the realization of the latter is Baqa, the resurrection. The soul, drawn by the magnetic power of the divine Spirit, falls into it, with a joy inexpressible in words, as a loving heart lays itself down in the arms of its beloved. The increase of this joy is so great that nothing the soul has ever experienced has made it so unconscious of the self; but this unconsciousness of the self becomes in reality the true self-consciousness. It is then that the soul realizes fully that 'I exist'".

What is the goal or the purpose of life and the creation of the world is the fundamental question that requires deep analysis and probe. People always ask questions like what one lives for and what one's objective in life should be. From the viewpoint of Islam, one would as well ask : "What is the objective and purpose of the creation of the world and what is the purpose of prophetic missions?"

The objective of there prophetic missions is similar to individual goals of people (Umma) for whom the prophets had been appointed; for, the prophets were sent to guide men towards certain goals.

It pertains to 'the goal of the Creator in Creation, the manifestation of His Will and Purpose. We cannot assume a goal for God, and believe that He wishes to attain something by his acts. But sometimes by the goal of creation is meant the goal of the created action, not of the Creator. This would involve the movement of the created towards perfection, not the perfection of the Creator Himself. In this sense, if we think that the nature of creation has always been movement towards perfection, then there is a motive in creation.

Naturally the mission of the prophets, too, is believed unanimously to facilitate man's perfection and to help him to remove the deficiencies which neither he, as an individual nor his society is able to remove. It is only with the help of their divine revelations that he can advance towards enhancing perfection.

Accordingly, every individual must recognize his potentialities and strive to realize them. This is the goal of our life.

Now we must go into detail : Whether the Qu'ran has discussed the goal of man, and whether it gives the reason for his creations as well as the mission of Prophets.

[The Qu'ran, Sura Al-Insan, Verse 3 : says, "We have shown man the way to be grateful or ungrateful." (76.3)][4]

But what is happiness according to the Qu'ran? It is often said that the purpose of man's creation and prophetic missions is to make man strong in knowledge and resolution, so that he may learn more and more, and secular the power to do what he desires.

Thus the purpose of a seed is to realize its potential to become a mature plant. Human's potentiality is much superior, he is meant to be knowledgeable and able. The more he knows, the more he can use his knowledge and the nearer he will be to his human goal and purpose.

Sometimes it is said that the goal of human life is happiness in the sense that during the time one is alive, he should live comfortably and happily enjoy the blessings of Creation and nature, suffer less pain from either natural causes or from fellow-creatures. This is considered happiness. This means, then, getting maximum pleasure and minimum pain.

It is also said that the prophets are sent to make it possible for man to secure maximum pleasure and have minimum pain. If the prophets have introduced the subject of the next world, it is meant as a continuation of this life. IN other words, as a way has been shown for human happiness and as following it requires the granting of a reward, and opposition to it involves punishment, this reward and punishment are presented on the models of this world, so that the laws of this world would not be futile. Moreover, as the prophets were in no position as executives in this world to grant rewards or deal punishment, another world had to be offered where the right would be rewarded, and the wicked punished.

But we come across none of these statements in the Qu'ran, where the purpose of creating jins and human beings is given as 'worship' [The Qu'ran, 51.56]. This may seem to us difficult to understand. Of what use is worship for God? It does not benefit Him. Of what use is it to man? But this point has been explicitly mentioned in the Qu'ran as the purpose of Creation. Contrary to the view that the next life is subsidiary to this one, the Qu'ran says: "If there were no Resurrection, Creation would be futile." And again it says : "Do you suppose that we have created you in vain?" [The Qu'ran, 23.115]

Is it assumed that creation is meaningless, and man does not return to God? In the verses of the Qu'ran the question of Resurrection occurs repeatedly with the matter of the rightfulness of creation. Its reasoning is based on the implication that this world has a god, and He does nothing in vain, and all is rightful and not in play, and there is a return to Him (The Sufix take this return as merging back with the Supreme Reality).

We come across very frequently with the idea in the Qu'ran that man is created in order to worship, and the worship of God is in itself a goal. If there is no question of knowing God, which is the prelude to worship, then man has failed in his advance towards the goal of creation, and from the viewpoint of the Qu'ran he is not happy. The prophets, to, are bent to guide him towards that happiness which is the worship of God.

Thus the goal and ideal that islam offers is God, and everything else is preparatory to it, and not of an independent and fundamental importance. In the verses where the Qu'ran mentions perfect human beings, or speaks on their behalf, it says they have truly understood the goal of life and endeavoured to attain it. It says for Ibrahim ("I have devoted my worship to Him who has created heaven and earth, and I am not a pagan"). [The Qu'ran, 6 : 80] This Sura, too, says : 'My prayer, worship, life and death are for God, who is the Lord of the Universe." [The Qu'ran, 6 : 163]

This monotheism of the Qu'ran is not merely an intellectual one, thinking that the origin of universe is one thing and its Creator is another. It includes the faith and conviction of man that there is only one Creator, and his goal, which is the only worthy one, is He alone. All other goals are the product of this one and subsidiary to it.

Thus, in Islam everything revolves round the axis of God, including the goal in the mission of prophets and individuals' goal of life.

The Qu'ranic concept of the life's goal differs in degrees but not in kind with that of the goals propounded by the Sufis. The difference is that the Sufis sees everything in God and God in everything. Like Shankara or like the Vedantins the Sufis are the propounders of the absolute realities. No doubt we can see the Shankara's theory of knowledge scattered here and there in the verses of the Qu'ran it is wrong to put them both on parallel axis.

Now let us study the question of worship. In the second verse, Ibrahim's words show pure devotion and he shows himself a thoroughly devoted servant of God who is ruled by no thought but that of God.

Concerning the reason for the mission of prophets, the Qu'ran offers several explanations. In Sura Ahzab, Verses 33, 45 and 46 it says : "O, Prophet, We sent you as witness, forerunner and giver of warning, to invite towards God by his leave, and to be a bright light." Thus a prophet is a witness to the people's deeds; a harbinger of the good deeds agent of warning against evil acts, and a man who calls human beings towards God, which is by itself an ultimate goal. Here from this verse it becomes clear that the ultimate goal of the creation is to merge with the creator.

Elsewhere a prophet's mission is mentioned as a duty to bring people out of darkness into light. So, it is clear that the people are called upon to know God. The prophets are the link between creatures and the creator.

In another verse another point is mentioned as the goal in the mission of the prophets : "Truly we sent our prophets with clear proofs and with them we sent the Book and true measure, so that the people rise in justice, and we sent iron in which there is great firmness and benefits for people..." [The Qu'ran, 57.25] In this verse by measure is probably meant law, so that justice will prevail. Thus, the prophets have come to establish justice, and this is another aspect of their objective.

According to the Qu'ran, man gains his happiness only from God, and it is he who fills all the gaps in his life, and satisfies him. The Qu'ran says : "Those who have faith and their hearts are tranquil in thinking of God, know that all hearts find peace by remembering God." [The Qu'ran : 13.28] Only God brings repose to the anxious and inquisitive hearts of man. Other things are subsidiary and preliminary matters, not the final stage.

The same is said of worship : "To remember God, pray." [The Qu'ran : 20.14]

Also, the following verse says : "Prayer checks wickedness and injustice, and remembering God is more important. "[The Qu'ran : 29.45] Islam thinks that man is created to worship God, to seek proximity to Him and to know him.

The goal of Islam is to be a perfect Muslim, and the perfect Muslim is one who realizes Allah in accordance with the norms set out for the common man as well as Salik (seeker after Truth). The common man's aim of life is to live this wordly life according to the Divine Law that is prescribed by The Holy Qu'ran and the Prophetic Traditions. The idea of a perfect human being is in fact basic Islamic ideal and forms the part of its ideology. The Islamic concept of the purpose of life can well be compared with four Purusharthas laid down by the Vedic Scriptures. In conclusion here we can say that the goal of life is not life negative but life positive. Almighty God (if taken the view as creator and creation) has given this life with certain purpose and those purposes are enumerated as divine laws in the scriptures with a motive to lead a moralistic life and there by either realizing or worshiping the God. The ultimate goal or purpose or meaning of life is to realize the God the Upanishads and the Sufis call the Brahman or the Self.

The Gnostics believe that the truth is the basis of everything. They say that the Truth is the Essence of God, and His manifestation is visualized in the shape of crated things and beings. Man, also as a more hearty creature gains perfection through his return to Him, (Sufis call this stage the Fana). Thus everything but truth which is God, is His shadow, while in itself it is a reality. God means absolute God, and nothing is equal to and comparable with Him, Sufis believe that man can attain unity with God, or, as they say, can be annihilated in His essence (Fana-fi Allah). Man is a being, separated from his originator, Man's perfection and happiness consists of his return to his origin in God's Essence. They also offer ways and means to attain this goal, and this lies through the whole of man's essence, that is, his heart and its changes and transformations, which remove the obstacles to perfect unity. Their means consist of love, worship and self-purification.

Philosophers, however, think differently, they consider man's essence to be his intellect, and other things are secondary matters, the perfection of the intellectual power has two aspects : speculative and practical. The speculative or theoretical aspect is wisdom which means the recognition of things as they are, and its practical aspect is justice, by which they mean that man's whole essence must be ruled over by intellect and not by instinct or other forces. Plato in his Theory of Republic points to a Utopia in which philosophers become rulers and rulers philosophers, This theory is also applied to individuals, and it is said that a man is happy when his essence is ruled over by philosophy, For them, attaining truth is not under consideration; they emphasize thought and reflection, not heart and spirit, The way to attain the goal is intellect, logic and reasoning.

Another group consider love to be human perfection, and that means forgetting self and loving others, so that there would be no boundary between self and others; and when there is a question of choice, others have priority over self. A being whose noble human sentiments have developed to their limit, may be considered a perfect being.

Chapter 6

Major Sufi Ascetics and Vedantic Influence Upon Their Thoughts

The history of Sufism begins with the history of Indo-Persian literature. In India Persian poetry started in the beginning of the fifth century of the Hijra (eleventh century AD) while KASHAFUL MAHJUB written by Data Ganj Baksh Ali Bin Usman AL Hujwiri is considered to be the earliest work of Persian prose in this country It occupies pride of place among prose works on Sufism and its author is the first Sufi writer of India.

The Sufis especially AL-Gazali and AL-Hujwiri claim that the doctrines of Sufism are solely derived from the Quran and the Hadiths (the prophetic traditions) but a close scrutiny of Sufi doctrines reveals that these doctrines do have the profound influence of extraneous mystical thoughts. The Sufism developed in India in the later period has a profound influence of Indian thoughts and Upanishadic philosophy. The early Sufis who have migrated from Arabia or Afghanistan to India first settled in the Punjab and Sindh regions of the Indian sub continent. They came in contact with many yogis and Upanishadic seers and have imbibed many mystical thoughts of these Rishis. The great Sufis of India were invariably men of deep learning and used to write in Persian as well as in various Indian languages while their discourses were mystic songs and couplets such as the songs of Rumi, Hafiz, and Sadi and the Bhajans and Garbis of Anwar kazi Sufism has reached to its magnificent zenith in India would have never reached to such heights even in its parent countries of Saudi Arabia had there not been an element of Vedantic mysticism merged into it. Sufism had originated in Arabia but it got nourishment, nurture and spiritual feeding in

India that is why today we find Sufism alive only in Indian sub continents. Had there not been India the haven for Sufi 'mystics and had there not been any encounter between the Sufis and Indian Rishis, Sufism would have died or would have become what now we see the wahabism in Arabia. Many Sufis like Hallaj-Mansur had come to India and had encounter with Indian Rushis. During the reign of Harun and Mamun the Abbasid Caliphs definite steps were taken to know Indian thoughts. During the reign of Caliph Harun-al Rashid systematic study of Indian thoughts began. There was a Hindu scholar named Bermark in the court of Caliph Harun al-Rashid. Under the auspices of Bermark the caliph is said to have sent Arab scholars to India to study the Indian scriptures. It was during this period that many Indian scriptures on a variety of subjects ranging from Religion, Philosophy, and astrology, to Science and Medicine were translated into Arabic language. In the early eleventh century Al-Muwaffik and Al-Baruni are said to have visited India for studying Indian thoughts. Al-Baruni had translated the Sankhya Darshan of Kapila, Yoga Sutra of Patanjali and The Bhagwad Gita into Arabic and it is till date considered authentic translations in the Arabic language. In the later periods during the reigns of the Mughals in India a synthesizing work of the two cults were done by Akbar the Great and his grandson Dara Shikoh. Dara shikoh had dedicated himself to the study of Hinduism. He translated the Sanskrit books into Persian and often he preferred the company of the Hindu mystics and Rishis. Dara Shikoh had translated the Ramayan, the Geeta, the Upanishads, and the Yogavashishtha. He translated the Upanishads under the Persian title as Sirr-e-Akbar. In translating the Upanishads he found profound knowledge in them. He extols the Upanishads as "the earliest of the Divinely books and the monotheistic streams." He compared the Upanishads with the Holy Quran and said that the hidden book mentioned in the Quran is none else but the Upanishads. The secret of the secrets or 'Ilmu-al Gaib' of Islamic Mysticism according to Dara Shikoh is the mystery of the Upanishads. These earlier and later encounter of the mystics and Sufis form the core of the development of pantheistic and absolutist ideas of Brahman in Sufism. These concepts are the concept of Fana and Moksha, Brahman and Allah, Wahadatul-

Wujud and Advaita, Suhuddiya and Nishprapanch Brahman, Tanazullat and Nirguna Brahman, Lataif and Chakras of Yoga.

The Upanishads talk about the Supreme Reality and to meditate upon this supreme Reality in the like manner the Sufis are also talking about to contemplate the Ultimate Reality by Dhikra and to attain unity with Allah. Hallaj's passion for this unity with the ultimate reality is exposed in his utterance of the words Anal-Haq that ultimately lead him to the gallows. It is said that Hallaj in his lifetime had come to India and had spiritual encounter with the Hath Yogis and the Rishis of India. This might have been the cause of Upanishadic reflections in his spiritual austerities and utterances.

Those Sufis who had come to India and had spiritual encounters with Indian Rishis had interwoven Indian mystical concepts in their practice but the Sufis who made India their home land nearly merged into Indian mysticism both Vedic and Tantaric. The Sufis of India like Baba Faridshad so become one with Upanishadic Rishis that their teachings reflect nothing but pure upanishadic philosophy. It is only because these saints did not recognize any distinction of or difference of any caste, creed, religion or gender in the path to Allah or Fana Fi Allah. This great saint Baba Farid had the credit of getting his verses interwoven into Adi Granth Sahib the holiest scripture of the Sikhism His verses interwoven into the Holy scriptures are still recited and reversed by Sikhs as well as non Sikhs. Baba Farid always talked about the Absolute Brahman and in his Sama, throngs of Hindus, Muslims Sikhs and others mingled together in Dhikra to unite with the Supreme Brahman.

The mystical verses of Baba Tahir another Sufi of India, the songs bhajans and Garabis of kazi Anwar a great Gujarati Sufi and many more had imbibed the true spirit of Indian Upanishadic mysticism. These saints do not make any distinction between Allah and Isvara or Brahman. They also talk that Atma is Parmatma. Like Shankaracharya many Sufis say that only Brahman is true all else except the Brahman is false and only because of Maya or false knowledge we cannot realize the Brahman. We can realize the supreme Reality or the Brahman by removing the veil if Maya that is false knowledge. This can be achieved through austerities and contemplation that is meditation in Indian mysticism and Dhikra in Islamic mysticism. Thus there seems to be the profound influence of Indian mysticism upon the Islamic mysticism. In this connection Sadhu Santideva says : "The Indian Mystic saints like Kabir Nanak and khwaja moinuddin Chisti and others and the adept of Radhaswami faith speak of advancement in the spiritual life as a journey (safar), the seeker after the Supreme Being a mureed or salik or musafir (traveler or pilgrim). The road as rah or path, the master as the trailblazer or pathfinder or murshid, guide or rehbar. The journey is from the part to the whole, from microcosm to macrocosm, from innumerability (anekta) to oneness or unity (ekta), from the realms of manas and maya to the universe of pure spirit (nirmal chetan desh), from the shell to the core, from the letters (alphabets) to the meanings, from physics to the metaphysics, from phenomenal to the nominal and beyond from duality to monism, from the three states of wakefulness-dream, and slumber through turiya (the fourth), sahasdal kanwal, the Turiyatit on to the twelfth state of hairat in the region of Haq (Sat Desh)."

Talking about the traveller on the path of Ultimate Reality he further says that, "the salik or the traveler is one who has taken to the ideal of ittihida or union with Radhaswami Dayal. He has accepted the batinia or the esoteric way, the way of tariqat as against shariat, the system of marifat divine knowledge or intuition, haqiqat as against batilat and was (union with Radha Swami dayala) through pure love ishq." In this way the salik or the seeker after truth can merge with Radha Sami dayal or the Supreme Reality.

Sufi Speculation Concerning God Compared with Brahman

The Sufistic concept of Allah is very similar to the Upanishadic concept of Brahman as vividly described in almost all the major Upanishads. The Upanishads talks about the Self and advise to contemplate or meditate upon the Brahman in the like manner the Sufi mystics do advocate the unity of the Self with the Ultimate Reality and ask to contemplate upon the Ultimate Reality. There are many concepts that go parallel with

Upanishads or rather Hindu Mysticism. The concept of Guru–Shishya corresponds to Pir and Murid, Wahadatul–Wujud with Advaita, Shuhudiya with Advaita of Ramanuja and Nishprapancha Brahman, Tanazulat with Nirguna Brahaman, fana with Moksha or Nirvana, and Lataif with Yoga Chakras. The concept and practice of Same (The Divine music) is interwoven into Islamic mystical practices from the Hindu rituals. Though music is forbidden in Islam the Sufi saints did include music and gave it the highest position in their Samas. The Muslim Sufis like Khwaja Moinuddin Chisti, Khwaza Nizamuddin, Khwaza Nasiruddin Chirage Delhi and Baba Farid all these Sufis upheld the same and included the people from all sects into their Samas. Hindus and Muslims all equally participated in the Dhikra of all these Sufis. All these great saints taught the non-dualistic philosophy of Advaita in their own version with some nuances but the ultimate goal of teaching and the unanimous voice remained the same that of Tawhid or unity of Allah. There were many Hindu disciples of the Sufis and there were many Muslim Shisyas (disciples) of the Hindu Guru. All these started in India in the prime time of the Bhakti Movement. The Bhakti movement started in India in 12th century by Ramanuja had a tremendous influence upon the Sufi saints of India. Hundreds of Sufis attracted by the cult of Bhakti started studying the Hindu scriptures and their mystical thoughts. Sindh was the most important center where Sufism mingled with Hinduism shined like stars in the sky. Many notable saints of this period were Shaikh Usman known as Shahbaz Qalandar, Shaikh Fariduddin Ganj-e-Shakar, Shah Inayat, Khwaza Muhammed Zaman, Shah Mir, Nanak Yusuf, Dalpat Ram and Sufi Paruram and his disciple Fakir Gopaldas Miskin. All these saints visited the golden temple in Amritsar and inspired by the teachings of Sikhism and Hinduism Baba Farid wrote many slokas (verses), which are included in the sacred book of the Sikhism. The Sufis of India were especially affected by the Bhakti movement and the teachings of Upanishads included them in their work.

All these saints whether Hindus or Muslims, men or women the inner spirit of their teaching is the same. They always preached equality, love, brotherhood, and unity of Allah or the

Supreme Reality. Let us see what various Sufis say in their teachings :

Lal Shahbaz Qalandar says :

I am falcon with no habitation
I cannot be contained in any place
I am phoenix with no trace
I cannot be contained in name.
At one time I wore the sacred thread.
At another I read the holy Quran,
Yet at another, I was in Christian religion.,
I have worn two hundred dresses.

Here the mystery of the Universal self enshrined in the arcane and labyrinth of various religions is reflected. The saint experienced or tasted every Religion but he found that the reality is one and the same.

Reflecting upon the Ultimate Reality and the realization of the Truth what happens to the mystic is beautifully uttered by Khwaza Muhammed Zaman in the following words :

Friends, every thread is cotton,
Kill not Mansur
When the phenomenal existence disappeared
He talked of An-al haq.[2]

The mystery of all religions lies in the unitariness of the absolute Reality. Revealing the hidden message of the Tawhid mingled with the Upanishadic touch Sachal says :

"Strike the Mulla on his fate
Yes on his fate
Some say this some say that
I am what I am
Some call me momin, some Kafir
I am what I am
I am not made of earth or air or fire or water,
Not am I born of any human parents
Why ask Sachal lineage, my name is unknowable."[3]

Bhai Dalpatram talks about the universal message of all Religions :

If there is one God in peepul tree and another in babul?
If Islam was created by Allah
Then who created Kufr
If ka'ba be the house of God
Why find faults with the idol temples?
The same light burns within the temple and the mosque.[4]

Nunao says :

Realize thyself first and then read Quran
Ram and Rahim are one, remove thyself
From in between
It is for love sake that I manifested myself,
I came on earth to see oneself.
From the spaceless I entered into space
Placing on my head the trust of love.[5]

We can find the traces of the Vedic and Upanishadic thoughts in the work, teachings and practices of the Sufi saints. In the above we can see the flowers of the Katha, Kena, Mundaka, Mandukya, Aitariya and Taittiriya Upanishads. In the teachings of the Sufis we vision the beauty of the Brahman as if we are on the journey towards God (sayr ila llah). As we have seen that this interaction of Hindu Yogis with the Sufis is not the one way interaction. It was a two way process. The influence of the Persian poet Hafiz on Maharaja Devendranath Tagore (the father of Gurudev Ravindranath Tagore) was so immense that we can see the devotional bell in the Shanti Niketan even today adored with the couplets from the Diwan of Hafiz Maharshi Devendranath was so eclectically learned that some Muslims called him as Jabarjast Maulvi[6]".

There are numerous analogies and similarities between the Sufistic or Islamic mysticism and the Hindu Mysticism. The Hindu concept of Moksha can well be compared with the Fana of Sufism. Moksha literally means release, and it is used in the Upanishads to indicate the release of the individual soul from the bondage.

Major Sufi ascetics and their mystical thoughts

Islamic mysticism that is Sufism has its origin in the very foundation of Islam. The ways the prophet ﷺ behaved and solved the problems of day-to-day life of the people who approached him has become the Hadith the compilations of code of conduct. In the days of the prophet ﷺ when he was alive whenever any question social, religious or cultural arose people approached the Prophet ﷺ for solution and the Prophet ﷺ answered them. The Tariqa of the prophet ﷺ was different and the answers varied according to the situations and circumstances of the time. Sufism in its present form or what we know today did not exist in the days of Prophet Mohammedﷺ.

However it was in existence in its true spirit in the life and conduct of the Prophet ﷺ and his associates. It was non existent only in name. It was existent without a name of Sufism. The Sufism that we know today developed early in Mesopotamia, Arabia, Iran, and Afghanistan especially in Khurasan, Sinai, Kufa, Baghdad, Basra, Cairo, Damascus and Balkh. The early Sufis are Hasan Basri, Malik-ibn-Dinar, Sufyan-a-Thauri, Maruf AI-Karkhi, Muhasibi, Habib Azmi, Ibrahim Ibn Adham, Rabi' Al-Adawwiya, and Zul nun Misri. From the Indian subcontinent there are as many Sufi ascetics as there are regions and as there are languages. The Indian subcontinents with the advent of Islam in India flourished and developed to its zenith in early hey days of Islam not because the Sufism in India got political protection but because the Sufi ascetics found many things that are eternal as similar to their practice. These Sufi ascetics imbibed many Tariqats from the Indian mystics and they imparted many mystical traditions to Indian mystics. It was not a one way process rather it was a multi way process. The concept of Dhikr is similar to Indian Yogic concept of meditation. The Sufi ascetics taken into this book are–Hallaj-Mansoor, Rumi, Rabi'a-al Adawwiya, Ain-al-Qudat-al-Hamdhani, Abdul Qadir Gilani, Shah Nimatullah, Sarmad, Khwaza Moinuddin Chisti, Nizamuddin Awliya, Baba Farid, Hazrat Pir Inayatkhan, and Shah Vajiuddin Alawi and Kazi Anwar.

The name Mawlana Jalaluddin Rumi stands for Love and ecstatic flight into the infinite. Rumi is one of the greatest spiritual masters and poetical geniuses of mankind and was the founder of the Mawlawi order of Sufism, a leading mystical brotherhood of Islam.

Rumi was born in Wakhsh (Tajikistan) under the administration of Balkh on 30th September 1207 to a family of learned theologian. Escaping the mongol invasion and destruction, Rumi and his family travelled extensively in the Muslim lands, performed pilgrimage to Mecca and finally settled in Konya, Anatolia, then part of Seljuk Empire. When his father Bahaduddin Valad passed away, Rumi succeeded his father in 1231 as teacher in religious sciences. Rumi 24 years old, was an already accomplished scholar in religious and positive sciences.

He was introduced into the mystical path by a wandering dervish, Shamsuddin of Tabriz. His love and his bereavement for the death of Shams found their expression in a surge of music, dance and lyric poems, 'Divani Shamsi Tabrizi'. Rumi is the author of six volume of didactic epic work, the 'Mathnawi', called as the 'Koran in Persian' by Jami, and discourses, 'Fihi ma Fihi', written to introduce his disciples into metaphysics.

If there is any general idea underlying Rumi's poetry, it is the absolute love of God. His influence on thought, literature and all forms of aesthetic expression in the world of Islam are beyond comparison.

Mewlana Jalauddin Rumi died on December 17, 1273. Men of five faiths followed his bier. That night was named Sebul Arus (Night of Union). Ever since, the Mawlawi dervishes have kept that date as a festival or Urs. Indeed Rumi was a great mystic, a Sufi and a poet in the path of Isqe Allah. His poems are full of divine love and mystery, the love between Allah and the Self. Though there is no distinction between the Self and the Brahman in both Upanishadic and Islamic mysticism still however the mystics used to address the Supreme Reality as their bride and they as his groom or vise versa. The Mawlavi sect of sufism evolved out of this concept. The dervishes of this order dance in glee and ecstasy considering themselves as the bide of God. Another sect known as Suhagiya is also of the same concept. The dervishes of this order wear long costumes and whirl in ecstasy. The Suhagiya Dervishes present themselves as the (dulhans) brides of the lord. The mystical and divine love poems of Rumi are beyond encomiums. The followings are some of them :

What is to be done, O Moslems? for I do not recognize myself.
I am neither Christian, nor Jew, nor Gabr, nor Moslem.
I am not of the East, nor of the West, nor of the land,
nor of the sea;
I am not of Nature's mint, nor of the circling' heaven.
I am not of earth, nor of water, nor of air, nor of fire;
I am not of the empyrean, nor of the dust,
not of existence, nor of entity.
I am not of India, nor of China, nor of bulgaria, nor of Saqsin
I am not of the kingdom of 'Iraqian,
nor of the country of Khorasan
I am not of the this world, nor of the next,
nor of Paradise, nor of Hell
I am not of Adam, nor of Eve, nor of Eden and Rizwan.[7]

Here the Upanishadic tint is visible in every word of this mystical poem. What is Brahman or what is Self? The Upanishads describe this Brahman or the self as neti....neti not this...not that because the Brahman is beyond description. That indescribable into words into human language. It is the stage that happens spontaneously after deep dedication, Dhikra and severe austerities. When it happens it happens spontaneously without any effort. It happened to Christ and it happened to Krishan or Mohammed or Mansur or Rabia or happened spontaneously to Aiyn-al-qudat-al Hamdhani. When the mystical experience happen it lasts for a moment but its effect lasts a life time. The impression it leaves behind on the heart and mind of the seer is immense and words baffle the thoughts in describing such a sudden and abrupt ecstatic experience. It happened to Rumi when a Sufi dervish Shams of Tabriz comes in his life. Rumi utters spontaneously :

Come come
The beloved has arrived

The rose garden is blooming
Run and offer your life and the world
To the rising sun.[8]

Here Rumi finds the Supreme Reality in the form of Shams who becomes his spiritual soul-mate and Rumi renounces the mantle of Shariat and enters the higher state of spirituality. He becomes one with his Guru (Peer) and danced in spiritual ecstasy. The rising sun in the above line is suggestive of the spiritual ascending of the seer. The Divan-i-Shams is pregnant with ecstatic love poems by Rumi. The poems of the Divan are not ordinary love poems of flesh and blood they are the poems of Spirituality, the poems of mystical yearning, the pomes of Tawhid (unit with God) and they are the mystical mantras of the Upanishads and in Jami's words the Quran in Pahelvi. The Brahman is nowhere yet He is everywhere. It is concealed in our hearts. It is very arduous journey if one embarks upon in search of the Supreme Brahman. He remains traceless and placeless. Rumi very beautifully and succinctly says into following lines :

My place is the Placeless, my trace is the Traceless;
'Tis neither body nor soul, for I belong to the soul of the Beloved.
I have put duality away, I have seen that the two worlds are one;
One I seek, One I know, One I see, One I call.
He is the first, He is the last, He is the outward,
He is the inward;
I know none other except 'Ya Hu' and 'Ya man Hu.'
I am intoxicated with Love's cup, the two worlds have
passed out of my ken;
I have no business save carouse and revelry.
If once in my life I spent a moment without thee,
Form that time and from that hour I repent of my life.
If once in this world I win a moment with thee,
I will trample on both worlds,
I will dance in triumph for ever.
O Shamsi Tabriz, I am so drunken in this world,
That except of drunkenness and revelry
I have no tale to tell.[9]

Rumi is also the poet of love not ordinary or worldly love of flesh and blood but he was in love with Allah. This love is called Ishq-e-Allah. Rumi's love affair with the supreme Reality is reflected into his ecstatic poetry spontaneously closed out of his heart when he was in union with the Supreme Reality. In the following lines Rumi desiderates liberation :

Oh Beloved,
take me.
Liberate my soul.
Fill me with your love and
release me from the two worlds.
If I set my heart on anything but you
let fire burn me from inside.
Oh Beloved,
take away what I want.
Take away what I do.
Take away what I need.
Take away everything
that takes me from you.[10]

The imagary used in this utterance is supernatural not ordinary but divinely inspired. Here we can taste the utterances of the Upanishadic seers but the method employed by the mystic is that of lover and beloved. The aim is the one and the same but the approach or the way is slight different. Rumi talks of Reality in the form of love as under :

The lover's food is the love of the bread;
no bread need be at hand :
no one who is sincere in his love is a slave to existence.

Lovers have nothing to do with existence;
lovers have the interest without the capital.

Without wings they fly around the world;
without hands they carry the polo ball off the field.

That dervish who caught the scent of Reality
used to weave basket even though his hand had been cut off.

Lover have pitched their tents in non-existence :
they are of one quality and one essence, as non-existence is.[11]

I cannot prevent myself quoting voraciously from Rumi's work as it contained the whole treasury of mysticism of the world. There is the spirituality of the Vedas, the mysticism of the Upanishads, the teachings of the Quran and the Bible and the Torah. There is the poetry par excellence, spirituality at its zenith, and mysticism shrouded in a bridal shyness waiting for the Groom to remove the veil and become one forever. My heart is so filled with spiritual ecstasy and love towards Rumi that I cannot stop quoting but let me conclude by citing one more poem;

Suddenly
(yet somehow unexpected)
he arrived
the guest....
the heart trembling
"Who's there?"
and soul responding
"The Moon..."
Came into the house
and we lunatics
ran into the street
stared up
looking
for the moon.
Then-inside the house-
he cried out
"Here I am!"
and we
beyond earshot
running around
calling him....
crying for him
for the drunken nightingale

locked lamenting
in our garden
while we
mourning ring doves
murmured "Where where?"
As if at midnight
the sleepers bolt upright
in their beds
hearing a thief
break into the house
in the darkness
they stumble about
crying "Help!
A thief! A thief!"
but the burglar himself
mindless in the confusion
echoing their cries :
"...a thief!"
till one cry
melts with the others.
And he is with you
with you
in your search
when you seek Him
look for Him
in you looking
closer to you
than yourself
to yourself :
Why run outside?
Melt like snow.
wash yourself
with yourself :

ruged by Love
tongues sprout
from the soul
like stamens
from the lily....
Blunt learn
this custom
from the flower
silence
your tongue.[12]

The above poem is full of mystical allusions. Each word is potent and pregnant with sublime beauty of the Supreme Reality.

Anwar Kazi a Mystic from Gujarat

Anwar Kazi a Sufi mystic from the land of Gujarat a fountainhead of Hindu Muslim cultural and religious unity and integrity was born in Visnagar of Gujarat in 1842 on the auspicious Friday. His father's name was A'zamiya. The ancestry of Kazi Anwar links him to Quresh lineage in which the Prophet Mohammed ﷺ was born. His ancestors came to India from Arabia during the Muslim reigns in India and first settled in Delhi. In Gujarat, first they settled in Patan. He had in him the ascetic qualities and mystical insight from the beginning of his childhood. He passed most of his child hood days in seclusion either in remote places or in the cemetery especially in the cemetery where a saint is buried. He had under gone rigorous austerities and often went without eating. His main mission on earth was to unite with God and thereby preach the people of Supreme Reality. He was completely careless about his health and the social and material life hence on the appeal of one Mr. Hathising Chunilal he was convinced to come back and live in the mosque. He went to Hajj pilgrimage to Mecca in 1887. People came into masses to have his vision so tried of this he started living in a rented hut nearby the locality of the Harijans and continued his austerities and Bhajans. He never boasted of knowing the six philosophies or Yoga or Shankhya or Qur'an. He simply appealed people to take him as a poor servant of God and asked them to be simple, straight forward and egoless. He appealed them to unite in Bhakti of Hari the great creator of the cosmos. He was a true dervish on the path of Fana. In 1915 he fell ill and with meagre clothing went to Palanpur a village in Gujarat where ultimately he met with his bodily death and was set to rest forever. A grand mausoleum was built on the holy tomb of the dervish by his follower Nawab Sher Mohammed Khanji of Palanpur in his memory, which is till this date is being visited and venerated by both the Hindus and the Muslims.

Kazi sahib has left for us many Garbis, Bhajans, Gazals, and Eligies, Nashihats in Urdu and Gujarati and local dialects. These poems are full of divine beauty and grandeur. The devotional songs in which Kazi employs the words such as Krishna, Pataliya Shamaliya and Mohanji are full of divine beauty and magnificence. The mystical and devotional songs of Kazi Anwar describe the beauty of the Lord. There is the voice of the Upanishads coming from the heart of the mystic. The devotional Garbis (songs in praise of Hari) are full of supernatural knowledge. In the poetry of Kazi Anwar we find the confluence of Gyan Yoga, Bhakti Yoga, and Karma Yoga. The words gush out from the heart of the mystic like an incessant flow of the river in heaven. There is an absolute monism, Advaita, both Sagun and Nirguna Brahman and pure theistic monotheism of Islam in the 'Gulshane-Khushi' the one and only monumental work Kazi left for the people of the world. Kazi Anwar is propounder of realizing Brahman like Shankara at the same time he is also taking about the blessings and grace of the God hence there are traces of almost all the different philosophies developed in India. What he was stressing was realization of the Brahman by whatever means either through Bhakti or through knowledge or through karma. When he sees God everywhere we see him as a pantheistic, when he talks about Self realization we find in him the Upanishads and when he talks about karma we see in him the Karma yoga of te Bhagawad Geeta, and when he sings the devotional songs in praise of the Lord we view him as Bhakti-margi.

As it was said, of Rumi's Mathnavi that put you finger anywhere on any page of the Mathnavi and you will find something for you. So is the case with the devotional songs and Bhajans of Anwar Kazi. The treasury of the poems of Kazi have in them moral lessons for every human being. He shows us the path of non-dualism and that is also the path of the Tawhid the oneness of the Supreme Reality. The Muslims call the Brahman as the *Noor (light)* and the prophet ﷺ a particle of the *Noor* (light). Contemplating God and establishing oneness with Allah one can get liberation and when one realized the supreme Reality the outer garbs of casts, creeds, gender and religion drop automatically. One who realizes the ultimate Reality recognises no duality even in the worldly objects. The verses taken from his anthology of poetry Gulshane Khushi are self-explanatory. Some of them are as under :

[Samaj man mera re mat ho tu magroor
Jo magroori ayegi tuko hovega hakse dur
Samaj man mera re mat ho tu magroor]

Know the self thou do not be egoistic
Egoism will lead you away from thee.
Know the self thou do not be an egoistic

[Santo sat batlana re maine muze na jana jee
Nahi main Hindu nahi musalma nahi yogika chela re bhai
Santo sat batlana re maine muze na jana jee]

Saints...show us the truth, I did not know the Self.
Neither a Muslim, nor Hindu not an acolyte-yogi
Saints show us the truth, I did not know the Self

[Hamne Brahman bichara re, hamara panth hai nyara ji
Mala manka ham nahi phere, pustak granth bisara re bhai
Dham jatra ham nahi jave, bhatke nahi sansara,
Hamara panth hai nyara ji.

Here the poet is seen deeply affected by the Gyan Marg of the Vedanta. The mystic Kazi says that he does not believe in the so called or pseudo ritualistic religion. The mystic's religion is to merge with God. The seer here seems to have entered into the state of Marifa of Sufism where the garments of outer religions drop automatically. The mystic does not have to try to drop the garments of religious rituals but they fall automatically. This happened with Lord Mahavira when his garment fell automatically. In case of Mahavira the garments should be taken not literally but they should be taken symbolically. One has to drop garments of outward rituals this happens only to the seers. The way of the mystic is different that is why Kazi says "*hamaro panth he nyaro ji*!" He is least concerned with the Mosque, Temple, Scripture, outward wordly rituals and traditions.

Devi devta ham nahi puje pathara kaun bichara re bhai
Deval mandir ham nahi jave chhoda thakar dwara re bhai
Hamara panth hai nyara ji.
Gyan nav me bathke santo gyani ne bhav tara re bhai
Hamara panth hai nyara ji.]

We thought of the Brahman, the different is my way
No counting of rosary beads, the books I threw away....
Different is my way
Gods we do not worship pilgrimage we keep away
I do not go to mosques and temples
Have I left gurudwara.
Sailing in the boat of wisdom, we crossed the worldly bay
Different is my way.

[Kaya tari sathi vatlani? murakh man
Kaya tari sathi vatlani re? panch tatva ni kaya bani tari prani,
Tena manhi chetan avyo re
Kuamtjo ti avup tuamtjo sai avua
Tema te judai sani ani re? murakh]

How is thy body spoilt, simpleton
How thy body is spoilt?
Of five elements, thy body is made.
The self came in simpleton
All came from where you came.
Then why such separateness? simpleton

[Avo avo ne albela[13] *mara mahole avo re*
Daasi jani ne dayalu daya dil ma lavo re]

Come...come oh...Dandy, come to my place
Take me thy odalisque and with thy mercy bless

Here the mystic poet invites the lord and urges Him to grant his wish. The mystic offers the Hari as His Daasi and appeals Him to bless with benediction. This has remained the way of the Sufi mystics. They offer them as servants in the way of God. Some Sufis offer themselves to the lord as their brides while some love God as their beloved or bride. The Suhagia Sufis or dervishes wear female garments, bangles, spangles, and tie pommels and roses in their braid and dance in ecstasy beating the drums. They say that they are the Dulhans of the Lord. In Gujarat the poet Dayaram has shown us the way of worshiping the Lord Krishna by becoming his Gopi. Here the point is that the female instinct in the worship leads one very close to God. As the wife's love of her husband never ceases, as the mother's love towards her child never decreases because there is a tender female feelings. In the same way, the female feelings or love towards God never decreases even in adversities.

[Hamne sodhi kaya re.. bhed antar ka paya ji
Eka eki unmuni[14] *hokar sohang shabd ranakaya re bhai]*
We found the body and fond the mystery of inner being
Establishing oneness (with Lord) in silence we uttered the word
[Tera khoj kiya tan mein tu akar chhupa mere manmein
Gokul mathura kashi dhundha, dhundha brindavan mein re bhai
Tu akar chhupa mere man mein.
Mandir aur masita dhundhi, na dekha mohan mein
Heera panna manak dhundhe moti ki malan mein re bhai
Tu akar chhupa mere man mein
Akhand jyot ka ajvala mein nirakh liya nainan mein.
Antar khoja darshan paya parakh liya chetan mein re bhai
Sad gugu charan mein shish namaya man mein hua parsan mein re bhai...
Tu akar chhipa mere man mein.]
Teri akalit maya re bhed koi ne nahi paya ji
jo samjya so diwana re jo murakh so dahya re bhai
Tera bhed sabhi nyara re tere bin nahi kisise yara
Ek lakh chovish hazar paygambar the tuje pyare re bhai
Kabhi jage tu jane re, par sabke raste nyare re bhai...tera bhed
Chobis tirthankar Jain ho gaye unka aur tha khaasa[15] *re bhai*

Ekso aath avtar kaha gaye unka juda tamasha...tera bhed
Gyani A' raf aur vahevari Shara' Sufi salik re bhai[16]

The mysticism reigns to its zenith in the poems of Anwar kazi. He addresses the Supreme Reality by different names. When he addresses the Reality by words such as Shamaliya, and pataliya we can see the bhakti of the Vaishnavites reflected in his poems.

Mansur al-Hallaj–A mystic martyr of Islam

Mansur al-Hallaj was born in the southern Iranian community of Tur in the province of Fars around 858. His full name was Abu Al-mughith Al-Husayn IbnMansur AL-Hallaj. He was a Sufi and one of Islam's most controversial writers, mystics, mystical and teachers. Because he was the embodiment of the Muslim experience, Mansur's life and death represent to many, a reference point in Islamic history.

His grandfather was a Zoroastrian, and was rumored to have been a descendant of Abu Ayyub, a companion of Muhammad. After relocating to a region famous for textiles, his father became a Muslim and may have made living by selling wool. Their family business was that of wool carder.

AI-Hallaj was fascinated with the ascetic way of life at a very young age. He memorized the Qur'an during his youth, and began to retreat from the world together with other like-minded individuals to study Islamic mysticism.

He later married, and made a pilgrimage to Mecca, and stayed there for a year. He began to travel the world abroad, preaching, teaching and writing along the way about the way to an intimate relationship with God. By the time he went on his second pilgrimage to Mecca, several apprentices accompanied him, and after returning to his family for a short period of time, travelled to India and Turkistan to spread the islamic teachings. After this, he made a third pilgrimage to Mecca, and returned to Baghdad.

The situation in which al-Hallaj taught and wrote was shaped by social, economic, political, and religious stress, which eventually led to his arrest. Sufism was new at the time, and it had provoked extensive opposition from the Muslim orthodoxy.

Sufi masters considered his sharing the beauty of mystical experience with the masses undisciplined at best, disobedient at worst. A combination of things probably led to his execution : he was an outspoken moral-political reformist.

AI-Hallaj was considered an "intoxicated Sufi," who became so enraptured in ecstasy by the presence of the Divine that he was prone to a loss of personal identity, which blurs the lines between the Divine and the Man. During his arrest he experienced one of these breaks and uttered : "An-al-Haq," or "I am the Truth" (or God). The statement was not only highly inappropriate in Islam, but echoed the philosophy of the Qarmatians[17]. Those three little words became the cause of the end for AI-Hallaj. His trial was lengthy and marked with uncertainty.

He spend 11 years in confinement in Baghdad, and was finally brutally tortured and crucified. Many witnesses stated that al-Hallaj was strangely serene while being tortured, and sincerely forgave his persecutors. He is referred to as "Love's Prophet". But here the love must be taken as Ishq-Allah love towards the God or the Supreme Reality. In this sense Mansur was really a love's prophet.

Today Hallaj is one of the most influential Sufi and an important character in Islamic history.

> *"I have seen my Lord with the eye of my heart, and I said: "Who are you? He said" 'You.'"*

Hallaj was hanged to death on March 26, 922.

Hallaj's mystical doctrine or utterances can be summarized as :

The Declaration of Unity

1. He is Allah the Living, the permanent
2. Allah is One, Unique, Alone and testified as onem and only.
3. Both are one and the consciousness of Unity of the One is in Him and from Him.
4. From Him comes the distance that separates others from His unity. He represented this mystery as :

 [18]

The horizontal line crosses the Arabic letter dāāl represents the mystical life of the seer. One has to cross many veils of ignorance by rigorous exercise, penance and contemplation. The Hallajian Sufis concentrate on such diagrammatical representation and starts Dhikra. This practice is still followed in India by Nath Yogis and Hath Yogis. Such focusing on mantra or letters resembles Indian mystical tradition.

5. The knowledge of Tawhid is an autonomous abstract cognizance.

   Symbolic presentation :[19]

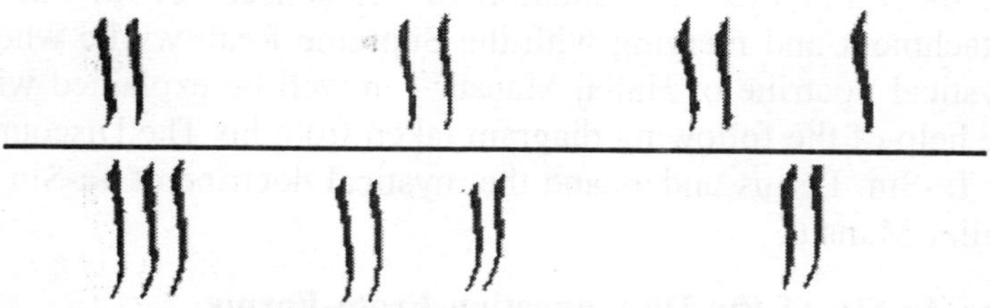

The Arabic letter alif in union of two is placed on and under the horizontal line. Alif represents the primordial essence al-dhat in the words of Jilli while daal represents its attributes.

6. The Tawhid (oneness of God) is an attribute of the created subject who utters it, and it is not an attribute of the Object professed as one.
7. If I being created say 'I', did I make Him also say 'I'? (wonderful mystery shrouded in this diagramatical representation.) My Tawhid comes from me then, not from Him. He is free (munazzah) of my Tawhid and me.
8. If I say 'The Tawhid returns to the one who professes it' then I make it a created thing.
9. If I say 'No, the Tawhid comes from the Object it testifies to', then what relation attaches the unifier to his profession of Unity?

10. If I say 'Then the Tawhid is a relation which attaches the Object to the subject,' then I have turned this into a logical definition.

11. The Tawhid is separate from Allah, and this symbol of wahadhiya is represented by alif with several daals in it. The alif being the Essence and the *daals* the Attributes.

12. **The uniqueness :** The primordial alif of the essence with the other alifs, which are the created forms, subsists on the primal alif incorporates the Islamic concept of Tawhid in its essence.

The Ta Sin of the disconnection from form : Hallaj in his Ta Sin of disconnection of forms explains the nature of the Self and how to be one with the Supreme Reality. The following is the diagrammatical presentation of his concept of Ta Sin of detachment and merging with the Supreme Reality. The whole mystical doctrine of Hallaj Mansur can well be explained with the help of the following diagram taken from his The Discourse on Ta-Sin. Let us understand the mystical doctrine of Ta-Sin of Hallaj Mansur.

The Ta-Sin of the Disconnection-From-Forms

1. This is the circle of the allegory and this is the figure which represents it.[20]

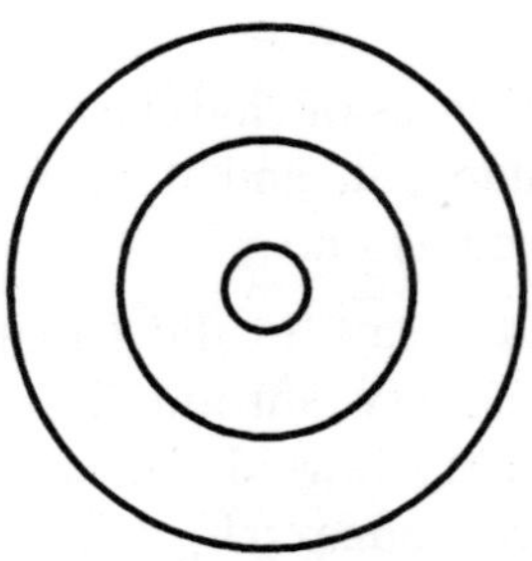

2. This is the whole which can give us phrases and sentences, and to the adepts, cults and sects, doctrines and methods.
3. The first circle is the literal sense, and the second is the inner sense, and the third is the illusion.

4. This is the totality of things, created and composed, answered, trodden upon, seized on, contradicted, deceived and stupefied.
5. He circulates in the pronoun 'we' of subjects of persons. Like an arrow he penetrates them, provides for them, surprises them, and overturns them, and He amazes them in crossing them.
6. Here is the totality of created substances and qualities. Allah has nothing to do with these fables.
7. If I say : 'He is He,' that statement is not the Tawhid.
8. If I say that the Tawhid of Allah is valid, they will tell me–'no doubt!'
9. If I say 'without time,' they will say : 'Then is the meaning of Tawhid a simile?' But there is no comparison when describing Allah. Your Tawhid is without relation to Allah or to creation, because the fact of expressing the number of times introduces a limiting condition. In so doing you have added a sense to Tawhid, as if it were contingent. However the contingent is not an attribute of Allah. His Essence is unique. And both Truth and what is unreal cannot emanate from the Essence of the Essence.
10. If I say : 'The Tawhid is the word itself," the word is an attribute of the Essence not the Essence itself.
11. If I say : 'Tawhid means that Allah wishes to be One' the diving volition is an attribute of the Essence and volitions are created.
12. If I say : 'Allah is the Tawhid of Essence proclaimed to itself,' then I make the Essence Tawhid which can be spoken by us.
13. If I say : 'No, it is not the Essence,' then do I say that Tawhid is created?
14. If I say : 'The name and the object named are One,' then what sense does Tawhid have?
15. If I say : 'Allah is Allah' then do I say that Allah is the Essence of the Essence and that he is He?

16. Here is the Ta-Sin which treats of the denial of secondary causes; and these circles with 'no' written in them are its figure.[21]

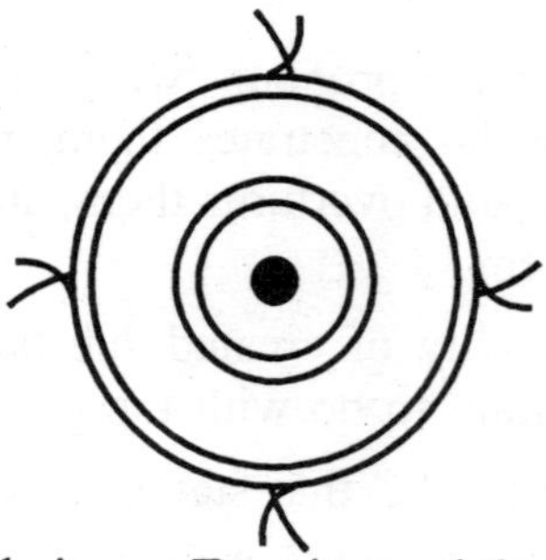

The first circle is pre-Eternity, and the second intelligible, the third is that of dimensions and the fourth of the cognizable.

17. The Essence is not without attributes.
18. The first seeker opens the Door of Knowledge and does not see. The second opens the Door of Purity and does not see. The Third opens the Door of Comprehension and does not see. The fourth opens the Door of Meaning and does not see. None say Allah in His Essence nor in his volition, nor in speech nor in His he-ness.
19. Glory to Allah who is holy and by His sanctity inaccessible to all the methods of the Gnostics and to all the intuitions of the people of revelations.
20. Here is the Ta-sin of Negation and Affirmation, and this is its representation :

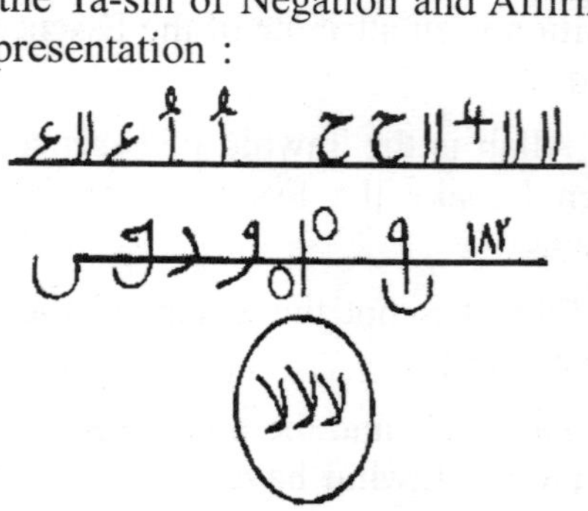

21. The first formula treats the thought of the common people and the second of the elect, and the circle which represents

the knowledge of Allah is between the two. The 'no's' which are enclosed by the circle are the negation of all dimensions. The two 'ha's' are set like pillars of other two sides of Tawhid which holds it up. Beyond them the dependencies begin.

22. The thought of the common people plunges into the sea of images and the thought of the elect into the sea of understanding. But these two seas dry up and the ways which they marked are effaced, the two thoughts disappear and the two pillars fall and the two words of being perish and proofs and knowledge vanish.

23. On the side of the pure divinity of Allah, he remains, transcending all dependent things, praise be to Allah who is not touched by any secondary cause. His proof is strong, and his power glorious. He, the Lord of Splendour and Glory and majesty. The Unaccountable one with arithmetical unity. No definition nor counting nor beginning nor end touches Him. His existence is a marvel since He is removed from existence. He alone knows Himself, Master of Majesty and magnanimity. Creator of souls and bodies.

Hallaj had left for us many mystical writings but most of them are lost or destroyed. This fool of God was crucified for the charges of heresy and blasphemy by those on the path of Shari'a.

Shaikh Abul Karim Jili : Jili believes that this world is like an iceberg and the light like God is like water which is the root of ice. Jili holds that being is one and that all visible or ostensible variations or differences are nothing but modes, aspects or manifestations of the one and the same Reality. The phenomenal world is the outward expression of Reality. He defines essence as to which names and attributes are referred. It may be either existent or non existent. It may be existing only in name like the mythical bird phoenix. Jili maintains that the essence that really exists is of two kinds : Pure Being and Being attached to not–Being that is the world of created things. The essence of God is indecipherable. He further stresses that to know this quintessence one has to strive through rigorous religious penance and Dhikra–the divine contemplation. Still however the essence of God is not revealed. It is known only through the attributes.

Pure Being has neither name nor attributes. Only when it slowly descends from its absoluteness and enters the region of manifestation names appear embossed on it. The totality of these attributes is the universe which is phenomenal. And that is also in the sense of Reality under the garbs of externality. Although at this point the distinction between essence and attributes is accepted, the two are ultimately one and the same. They are always united together as one cannot separate clay from the pot.

Rabi'a : The mystic woman in male dominated society

Rabia is the most dignified female Sufi in the history of Islamic Mysticism. Without Rabia the edifice of Sufism even of Islam will collapse like a palace of cards. Rabia has sacrificed a lot in the way to Allah. She was totally absorbed in the Supreme Reality but this Seer is now forgotten totally as the Wahabi movement has started false propaganda against the Sufism and the Sufis. It is because of their lack of knowledge and understanding or rather God known reasons that they are speaking against Sufis and Sufism. Rabia was a great mystic and She shall remain forever in the hearts of the mystics. The following are the words of Rabia and I would like to begin with these words.

'Your hope in my heart is the rarest treasure
Your Name on my tongue is the sweetest word
My choicest hours
Are the hours I spend with You–

O God, I can't live in this world
Without remembering You–
How can I endure the next world
Without seeing Your face?

I am a stranger in Your country
And lonely among Your worshippers :
This is the substance of my complaint.[22,]

Rabia was a mystic, or a saintly woman, who spent her whole life in devotion to God. She was born approximately in 717 AD, in the city of Basra, in Iraq. She came from a poor family. She and her three sisters suffered very much, for their parents had died and then there was a great famine.

It was a vicious and hazardous time. The starvation made people brutal, ready to do almost anything to survive. Rabi'a knew it was not safe to walk alone in the town, but she had to find food. One evening, she slipped out of the house into the street. Suddenly, someone caught her, holding her roughly. A hand was over her mouth–she could not cry for help. She had been captured by a wicked dealer in slaves, who then sold her in the market, for just a few coins. As a slave, Rabi'a served in the house of a rich man. She had to work hard, for long hours. Yet all the time, through out the day as she worked, she prayed and fasted/ Even at night, she slept little. She often stood praying as dawn broke and her daily task began.

One night Rabia's master found her praying so that he could not sleep He got up, and walked over to the window of his room. He looked down, into the courtyard below. There, he saw the solitary figure of Rabi'a, his slave. Her lips moved in prayer, and he could just catch the words in the still night air. Oh God, Thou knowest that the desire of my heart is to obey Thee, and if the affair lay with me, I would not rest one hour from serving Thee, but Thou Thyself has set me under the hand of Thy creature. 'For this reason I come late to Thy service.'

There was something very strange about the scene. At first, the master could not quite understand what it was. Then he realized. There was a lamp above Rabia's head. It hung there, quite still–out without a chain. As he watched, its light filled the whole house. Suddenly, he was afraid. He returned to his bed, and lay awake, thinking of what he had seen. He was certain of only one thing. Such a woman should not be a slave.

In the morning, he called Rabi'a to him, and spoke to her kindly. He told her he would set her free. "I beg your permission to depart," murmured Rabi'a, and her master agreed at once. Rabia set off out of the town, deep into the desert. There she lived as a hermit, alone for awhile, serving God. Later, she went to Mecca as a pilgrim.

The Main Sufi Orders

Hujwiri in his 'KASHF AL MAHJUB' describes eleven different Sufi orders by citing 'ABU HASAN NURI'. These eleven sects are as under :

01. The MUHASIBIS
02. The QASSARIS
03. The TAYFURIS
04. The JUNAYDIS
05. The NURIS
06. The SAHLIS
07. The HAKIMIS
08. The KHARRAZIS
09. The KHAFIFIS
10. The SAYYARIS
11. The HULULIS

There are as many Sufi orders as there are geographical places or regional languages but according to Abu Fazal there are main four orders of Sufism prevalent in India and I shall concentrate only on these four orders of Sufism.

These four orders or Silsilas are :

01. The Chishtiya order
02. The Quadiriya
03. The Soharavardiya
04. The Naqshbandiya

Among all these Sufi orders the Chistiya and the Quadiriya are the most well known and dominant orders in Indian sub continents and there are larger number of followers of these two sets. As we know that in India Sufism is widely influenced by Vedanta it is worth while to discuss in detail these four orders.

The Chistiya Order

The order is found by Khawaja Moinuddin Chisti' in India but its origin goes back to Khwaja Abu Ishaq Shami Chisti. Khwaja Moinuddin Chisti was born around 1142 AD and came to Delhi in India in 1192 with the invading army of Sahabuddin Ghori. He moved to Ajmer in 1195 AD when he was 52 years old where he lived till his death 1236. His Dargah (Mausoleum) has become a "Kaba-O-kashi" for thousands of Hinds and Muslims. Khwaja's philosophy of mysticism is akin to vedantic philosophy of mysticism. He talks about Wasl (Union) with the ultimate reality. After his death Chistiya order in India was continued by his murids and successors such as Qutbuddin Bakhtiyar Kaki, Baba Farid-uddin Ganj Shakar, Nizamuddin Auliya and Makhdum Alauddin Ali Ahmed Sabir of Pirane Kaliyar. The chisti order the west world is carried on by Hajarat Pir Inayat Khan who belongs to Nijami Branch of Chisti order. Peer Inayat khan was born in Baroda and he was a Gifted musician he used to play flute on the occasion of Ganesh Chaturthi a festival of Hindus. Inayat khan's musical talents were molded by his meternal grand father Maula Baqsh who was the chief founder of Gayan shala (The Academy of music) in Baroda with patronage of Maharaja Sayajirao Gayakwadd. Peer Inayat khan was master of many languages including Arabic, Urdu, Persian and Sanskrit. He left India for America in 1910 and stayed there until 1912 then he went to France, England, and Russia and finally stayed in England until world war Ist. Then he settled in Paris. He came back to India in 1926 and he died 5th February 1927 in Delhi and he was buried in Nijamuddin near the dargah (shrine) of Nijamuddin Aulia. There were other prominent Sufi mystics of the Chistiya order such as Kutbuddin bakhatyar kaki, Baba Farid, and Hadrat Sabir of Kalyar. It is mot important to state here that these Sufis particularly Nizamuddin awliya and kutbuddin preferred to remain away from the state affairs. Despite a generous offer from the state to give them status they did not accept it. Instead they tried to keep themselves distant from the king.

The life and thought of Moinuddin Chisti was characterized by a Unitarian and humanist world view. He would say that one who recognizes God is known by his separation from the creation and solitude in gnosis. Recalling bastami, he observed that, "when we come out of the skin like a snake, we saw the lover, the beloved and love as one. That is the world of Unity all is one (dar'alam-i-tawhid hama yak yist.)"

The Chistiya branch of Sufism is well known not only in Indian subcontinent but in the entire world.

There is a large number of followers of this branch of Sufism in the Indian sub continent. Followers of both the communities equally worship and seek for help and blessings by visiting Khwaza Moinuddin's Shrine in Ajmer. This is because of a synthesis the Khwaza Garib Nawaz (as he is fondly well known) made of different religious traditions and culture in his teaching. Shuja Alhaq notes in his *"Forgotten vision"* by citing Lawrence that, 'the social climate of Rajasthan was indifferent to Islam and probably hostile to its outspoken propagators." He further adds by citing Nizami that, 'the horrible environment of caste system where Moinuddin put forward the doctrine of Unity of God and equality of human beings was a great success.' Here I would like to drive home the point that the false propaganda in India is now on swing that Islam was spread in the world particularly in India by the might of the sword does not hold water. The Sufis (I would like to address them with a title the true Momin) spread Islam not by sword but by synthesizing the principles of all religions into their teachings. Khwaza Moinuddin had the disciples from all religions and his Sama was attended by the people of all castes and creeds with equality. The dress code of the Sufis of Chistiya branch resembles to that of the dress code of the Yogis. One can see even today that the Khadims of Moinuddind's shrine in Ajmer wear the saffron dress resembling the dress of a yogi. This is the beautiful outward synthesis of the two cultural or religious traditions. Khwaza had great respect and reverence for the Hindu devotions mingled with sound of Conchs. It may be true because when the prophet Mohammed was asked how he felt when he received the first message from Allah. He recalled that it was like the sounds of the ringing bells. I would also like to focus on the false notion of conversion being labeled against the saint. The mode of teachings of the Sufis was not that of converting people's faith rather the mode was to unite them together by shedding away false ritual practices and dogmas that have occupied the minds and hearts of the so called religious people. The other Sufis and disciples and successors of Khwaza Moinuddin Chisti were, Khwaza Kutbuddin Bakhatyar kaki, Hamiduddin Sufi, and Nizamuddin Awliya. The simplicity of Hamiduddin Sufi is beyond comparison. He was just like a typical Indian farmer tilling his small farm in Suwal near the city of Nagor in Rajasthan. He propagated pure vegetarianism to his disciples. He warned his disciples not to slaughter animals after his death and offer them as libation for seeking blessings. Animal slaughtering according to Hamiduddin Sufi was a sinful act and Allah never permits anybody to kill animals for his personal ends. The beautiful creation of Allah is not there to be destroyed. If we cannot create we must not destroy he used to say in his daily prayers.[23]

Hazrat Nizamuddin Awliya was another great Sufi from Chisitiya branch after Khwaza Moinuddin and Khwaza Kutbuddin Kakai. He emphasized on devotion and sincerity rather than formal ritual prayers, he suggested that a man too much obsessed with the religious duties might have some guilt to hide or some other need to compensate for.

2. Qadiriya Order

The Qadirya order branch of Sufism is founded by Sheikh Abd-al-Qadir-al-Jilani born 1077–1166 AD in a small village called Nif or al-Jit in Iran. His name was Muhiyuddin Abu mohammed Abd-al-Qadir-al-Jilani but he was known by many titles and names such as, al-Gausul-Azam (Manifestation of Allah's attributes), al-Qutb-al-Azam (The summit of spiritual evolution) and Mehboob-al Sub-hani (The most favoured by Allah). He lost his father when he was in his childhood. The qualities of spirituality started evolving in him from his early childhood days. He got initial knowledge of the basic religion from his mother. He was very truthful from the very days of his child hood. The story of revealing the moneytied under his garments on the loin to the thieves reflects his truthfulness and discipline imposed upon the child by his mother. His mother advised him to be truthful even in adverse circumstances. At the age of 18 child Abd-al-Qadir-al-Jilani left Jilan for Baghdad in search of the master as his inward quest compelled him to embark upon the journey towards mysticism. He finished his study under Sheikh Abul Khayr Hammad ibn al Dabbas a saint who was illiterate but renowned for his spiritual excellence. It is said that one Hambali Qadi Abu Sayed Mubarak al Mukhrrimi initiated him into the mystic fold. After his academic and spiritual study, he spent eleven years in seclusion without any human company. The seclusion developed in him the mystical attitude and slowly and steadily he became the Sufi par excellence. Reflecting upon the hierarchy prevalent in Sufi orders it is said that the one on the highest throne control the world and that one who sits on the highest throne is called Qutb (Pole) in Sufistic language. ibn-Arabi says that Abd-al-Qadir-al-Jilani was a Qutb. Hujwiri says, "But of those who have power to loose and to bind and are the officers of the Divine Court, there are three hundred called Akhyar and forty called Abdal, and seven called Abrar and four called Nuqaba and one called Qutb or Ghawth." Abd-al-Qadir-al-jilani was the greatest the Qutb and the Ghauwth. He has to his credit many esoteric and mystical writings such as :

(1) Al-Gunyah li-talibi Tariq al-haqq (Wealth for the seekers) a wide ranging work on islamic way of life and duties.
(2) Al-Fath al Rabbani–a book of sermons.
(3) Futuh-al Ghayb–victory of the invisible.

The mystic chanting or Dhikra adopted by the Qadiriya branch is different than that of Chistiya branch of Sufism. There are different types of stroke with varied intensity. These strokes are important in raising the seeker's level of ecstasy while he is in complete control of his master. After rigorous Dhikra the Quadirya employs pasi-a-nafs that means regulation of breath that may allow the name of allah into the whole body and the body starts vibrating with each stroke of breath. This is to control the nafs or the bodily instincts or lower passions. This practice of the Qadirriya branch seems very similar to the yoga practice of Patanjali.

The mystical thoughts of Abd-al-Qadir-al-Jilani can be summarised in brief as :

On Creation of the World

Abd-al-Qadir-al-jilani believed that Allah most High first created from the divine light of his own beauty the light of Mohammed. "I have created the soul of Mohammed from the light of my manifestation." He believed that the soul of Mohammed is the essence of all beings, the beginning and the Reality of the entire Universe. Allah after the creation of the light of Mohammed created the throne, and then he sent the soul to descend the lower level of creation to the realm of the material world, to the realm of matter and body. Sura Tin of Quran says : "then we make him descend to the lowest of the low. After that he sent that light to the ultimate realm (alam-al-lahut) which is the realm of manifestation. The process goes on and on till it reaches to the creation of the spiritual souls. Then he caused them to descend to the world of matter, water, fire, earth and sky and they became human souls. From this world he created the bodies of flesh and blood."

Here also we can see the evolutionary process of the entire universe and the human beings very similar to the evolutionary process described in Vedantic literature.

Abd-al-Qadir-al-Jilani has reflected upon many aspects of life of this world and the life here after. He has discussed very profusely the mystical aspect of religion accompanied with the day to day significance of it in practical life of human being. His thoughts are purely based on the Quran and the Hadith literature but they are given the mystical diversion in Sufism.

Abd-al-Qdir-al-Jilani had a wide ranging followers in the world. The sect is named after him as Quadiriya. His mosoleum is in Baghdad Iraq were the Sheikh got his religious, spiritual and ascetic teachings and became the mystic of the highest rank.

The Suhrawardiya Order

The Sohrawardiya order is founded by Shaikh Shihabuddin Umar ibn Abdulla Suhrawardi (1144-1234). In this order the Pir or the guide asks first the disciple to repent for the sins of his past. Then he is directed to utter or recite the Shahada or Kalima. In India large number of followers of this order are found. The practice of Dhikra and teachings of this order are also based on the Quran and the Hadith of the Prophet. The seers under go rigorous austerities to climb the ladder of four stations and ultimately to merge with the Ultimate Reality.

Naqshbandiyah Order of Sufism

The Naqshabandidyan order or the Sufi silsila is founded by Khwaja Baha Uddin Mohammed Naqshband (1317-1389) a native of Bukhara. The Silsila of Naqshbandiyah first established in central Asia and from there it spread to different parts of the world especially Syria, Turkestan, Afghanistan and India. The credit goes to Khwaza Baqi-Billah in establishing a Naqshbandiyah order in India.

Spiritually, the Naqshnandiyah stand out visualizing a whole universe of spiritual experience and adventure. The mystical principles of Naqshbandiya order can be enumerated as follows :

(1) Hush dar dam : conscious contemplation of other Supreme Reality

(2) nazar bar qalam : regulating each moment for the divine cause.

(3) safar dar watn : introspection of the Self and merging it with fana fi Allah.

(4) khalwat dar anjuman : solitude when one is in company of internal solitute.

(5) yad kard : recollection of Allah

(6) baz gard; restraining the thoughts

(7) nigah dash; keeping vigilant for the lower passions and to be pure of heart.

(8) yad dash : Storing Allah in the memory as precious treasure

(9) wasl : Union with the Ultimate Reality.

Almost all the Sufi orders stress on contemplation and Dhikra and thereby seek union with the Reality. The methods they employ do differ but the goal remains the same.

There are as many Sufi orders as there are regions and as there are different languages. There are many small orders such as Lal Shabaz Shahi, Miya Khel shahi, Naushahi, Qubrawi, Rifai, Shabiri, Sattari, Hamza Shahi and so on and so forth. Today Sufism has remained only in name and is on the verge of extinction because the puritanical movement *i.e.*, Wahabism has started in full swing. The Sufis always preached love, brotherhood, and humanity towards all people. They allowed people from all creeds to attend their Samas. There was no discrimination on the ground of religion and race or gender. The flower of Sufism bloomed once in the past and spreading its fragrance all over the world which is till today spread aroma in the world. The Sufis of all periods of time and place imbibed the universal principals of all religions and interwoven them in their teaching. Because of the richness of thought and absence of discriminations of castes and creeds, Sufism reached on such greatest heights.

References

1. Sufism in Sindh Dr. H.I. Sdarangani.
2. *Ibid.*
3. *Ibid.*, p. 205.
4. *Ibid.*, p. 205.
5. *Ibid.*, p. 205.
6. Sufism in India S.A.H. Abidi.
7. Diwan-i-Shamsi Tabriz Rumi.
8. Hidden Music Rumi Translation Maryam Mafi.
9. *'Divan-i-Shams' Translation R.A. Nicholson.*
10. *Ibid.*
11. Mathnawi III, 3020-3024.
12. Diwan-e Shams, v. V.ED. FURUZANFAR, p. 2172.
    (translated by Peter Lamborn Wilson)
    The Rumi Collection, edited by Kabir Helminski.
13. Naughty of dandy youth.
14. Silent.
15. Method or the way.
16. *From Anwar kavya Gujarati.*
17. Qarmatians are declared by fundamentalists as atheist and their utterances are considered as blasphemy.

18. The Diagram is taken from ancient Urdu Book of commentary on Ta-sin of Hallaj Mansur.
19. The Diagram is taken from ancient Urdu Book of commentary on Ta-sin of Hallaj Mansur.
20. The Diagram is taken from ancient Urdu Book of commentary on Ta-sin of Hallaj Mansur.
21. The Diagram is taken from ancient Urdu Book of commentary on Ta-sin of Hallaj Mansur.
22. *From Door Keeper of the Heart Charles Upton.*
23. Usul-at Tariqa.

Chapter 7

Conclusion

The Vedanta literature is full of mysticism. The Upanishads spread before us the tapestry of mystical knowledge as the seers or the Rishis of the ancient era saw them coming out from the mouth of the Lord of the universe *i.e.*, Supreme Reality. It is the mystical nature of the Upanishads that they have occupied the pivotal position in the world. The mystical utterances or the Mantras are not merely the imaginary world of never never land, but they are potent with spirituality and tested with experiences of the learned and the Siddhas (those who have realized the Truth). The Upanishads shift the centre of interest from Vedic gods to the reality behind changing phenomena. Upanishadic seers turned the vision more inward and gave a new direction to the spiritual life. That permanent eternal and unchanging reality is called brahman or Atman, which is existence consciousness and bliss[1]. Upanishadic literature also concentrates on self the inner controller of man. It analyses the Self, and distinguishes between its outer layer and inner Reality. The real self is pure consciousness. Not being limited by anything, it is infinite. The real self is called Atman. Every one contains divinity within him and there is no difference between individual self and the Ultimate Reality-Brahman[2]. The 'Katha' Upanishad reveals the truth by stating that this self is concealed in all things, and does not therefore appear to be there but it is perceived by the keen sighted with the help of the sharp, penetrating intellect[3].

The Brahman, atman, the world (Samsara), liberation, Upasana (meditation) knowledge, law of Karma etc. are the main concepts of the Upanishadic literature. The seers of the Upanishads saw that everything in the universe changes and they called it the creation Samsara *i.e.*, which always moves or changes. They also perceived that behind these ever changing phenomena there is an unchanging supporting ground from which the changing worlds emanated like sparks from a great fire.[4] This supreme, all pervasive entity is called brahman. The Mundaka Upanishad gives a beautiful description of all pervasive nature of Brahman. It states that Brahman verily is the immortal being. In front is brahman behind is brahman, it is to the right and to the left. It spreads forth and above and below. Verily Brahman is this effulgent universe[5]. The passage from Svetasvetara Upanishad makes it very clear that although sages worshipped many manifestations of the Divine they realized that the Brahman is behind them all, "filled with Brahman floweth all that is." Everything emanates from brahman, yet it remains the same. Through changing universe, out side is pervaded by the Brahman, the changing world within man himself is based upon the unchanging, undying Atman. It is the body, states the katha Upanishad that is destroyed, not the self within the body. Chandogya Upanishad identifies this individual Self with brahman by setting that "that thou art." According to Upanishadic literature, the supreme goal of life is the realization or identity between the brahman and the Atman.

This idea of unity between supreme Reality and the individual self gave birth to one of the most important concepts of the Hindu Religion, that all human being, because of their common spirituality, are the members of a single extended family. Upanishads declare that all are "the children of immortality" (GOD). WE ARE ALL Children of that glorious one supreme consciousness, because we carry the light and power of the brahman within our consciousness.

Another important teaching of Upanishad is the essential unity of all religions and of all spiritual paths. It proclaims that the Truth is one non dual consciousness. Everything is pervaded by this highest principle. It is though nameless and formless; it is called by different names and worshipped in different forms by different people. Various Religions or faiths thus are different paths to the same goal. Different religions are like different rivers, which go to the same ocean.

Another feature of Upanishadic teaching is fearlessness from the death. It is significant to note that death is not a horror in Hindu Religion. It takes death as a natural process. According to Upanishads, in the state of realization, individual becomes aware of his deathless Self (Atman). The immortal prayer of the Upanishad is :

> *"from the unreal, lead me to the real,*
> *from the darkness lead me to the light*
> *from the death lead me to the immortality."*[6]

The doctrine of Karma is another concept of the Upanishads which constitutes the essential part of the Hinduism. According to this doctrine no one can escape action and once a person acts, is bound by it. Action may be good or bad, it is followed by pleasant and unpleasant consequences respectively. Hindu belief is that, individual self bound by his own action is born again and again until he attains liberation. A beautiful simile is used in Katha Upanishad *i.e.*, "like corn, a mortal ripens and like corn he is born again.[7]"

Upanishads are termed as the Himalayas of the Indian thoughts. Almost all Indian philosophical systems derive their substances from the Upanishads. All orthodox schools of Hinduism accept them as a revealed wisdom. The Bhagavad-Gita is considered as the essence of the Upanishads. The equally important Vedantic text, viz., the Brahma sutra of Badarayana is described to be the thread which strings together all the Upanishadic flowers. Even the Religion of Buddha, if rightly interpreted, is only continuation of their deepest intuitions. The remarkable dialogues between the teachers and the pupils of the Upanishads deal with the deepest problems of human existence, of the goal of life and the stages of spiritual realization. The following Upanishadic statement proves that they are effective means of spiritual realization : "The Omkara is the bow, the Atman or the Self is the arrow, the target is the Brahman, and one should understand the Brahman through discrimination and detached mind." Kaatha Upanishad inspires us to arise, awake, and move onwards across the sharpen razor-edged path of spiritual attainment.

The Upanishads teach us a lofty universal Religion. In this great literature we have a Religion, which cuts across the barriers of hatred and separatism that have been built in the name of the Religions. After studying the Upanishads the famous German Philosopher made a wonderful statement declaring that, "in the whole world there is no study so beneficial and so elevating as that of the upanishads. It has been the solace of my life; it will be solace of my deaths."

Upanishadic and Islamic Mysticism seems to be very similar because the Ultimate Truth or Reality is one and shall remain one and the same. The Truth remains unchanged and is not affected by spatio-temporality. The whole of the argument of the Upanishads is centred round the Self. This Self is called the Atman and this Atman is nothing but brahman himself. The Kena Upanishad begins by the question Kena that is by whom? Or who? Who is that sees through our eyes yet does not form the part of the eyes. Who is that speaks through our tongue yet is not tongue and who is that thinks but is not the part of the brain. The answer to these questions is one and only one that is the Self. It is the Self that is timeless eternal beyond death and beyond sense perception yet that Self is the locus standi of the human life. Whether it is Kena or Katha or Mandukya, or Brihadaranyaka or Aitareya or Taitiriya or Prashna or Mundaka all these Upanishads herald the supremacy of the self. All animate or inanimate things evolved spontaneously out of this Self. The Aiytariya Upanishad says :

Before the world was created, the self Alone existed; nothing whatever stirred. Then the self thought :

"Let me create the world[8]*"*

In a very beautiful yet mystical conversation the sage Yajnavalkya explains his wife Maitreyi about the ephemeral nature of the wordly things and advises her to concentrate upon the Self. Nothing is above death except the Self that is beyond the death and time. The sage says to his wife

You have always been dear to me,
Maitreyi, and I love you even more now that

You have asked me about immortality. Sit
Here by my side and reflect upon what I say.[9]

A wife loves her husband not for his own
Sake dear but because the Self lives in him.

A husband loves his wife not for her own
Sake, dear but because the Self lives in her.[10]

The arguments and the explanations with vivid illustrations go on and on until the sage says that as long as there is separateness as long as thee is duality the Self cannot be realized. As long as there is separateness one sees, hears and speaks another from oneself.

Both the Upanishads and the Islamic Mysticism though in quite contradictory terms declare the unity of the Self both the currents of Hindu-mysticism and Islamic mysticism are never life negative. They are life positive. They never negate the phenomenal world of transitoriness. Both the schools believe in the liberation of the soul and suggest ways and means to attain liberation. In this transient world one has to establish relationship with the world while keeping consciously detached from it. The great Sufi scholar Ibn-Arabi brilliantly expounds the right relationship with the world:

> *"This world is a place of preparation where one is given many lessons and passes many tests. Choose less over more in it. Be satisfied with what you have. In fact, prefer to have less."*[11]

Arabi further states :

> *"This world is not bad-on the contrary, it is the field of hereafter. What you plant here, you will reap there. This world is the way to eternal bliss and so is good-worthy to be cherished and be praised. What is bad is what you do with the world when you become blind to the Truth and totally consumed by the desires, lust, and ambition."*[12]

The Rishis of the Upanishads and the Sufis of Islamic mysticism have shown us the path how to realize the supreme Reality or the Brahman. The aim or the goal of both the paths also goes almost parallel."[13] Speaking about Islam it is to be remembered that before the advent of Islam there were 360 idols in the holy Kaaba and the pagan Arabs worshipped each idol a fresh for the each corresponding day of the year.

Among the 360 idols there were three Goddesses namely Al-Lat, Al Manat and Al-Uzza. They were called the daughters of Allah. Allah occupied a position of higher God whose duty was to give good rain and good crops and look after the cattles. Allah was not the Supreme Reality in the pagan Arabia. People worshipped different Gods on different occasions and killed each other in the name of religion when dispute arose regarding the matter of worship. Prophet mohammed did a great revolution in throwing out all these 360 idols from Kaaba as these idols were the bone of contention among the pagan Arabs. Sometimes it so happened that the pagan Arabs brought out their sabers and were ready to cut to pieces their brethren the fellow pagan Arabs only for getting the first right to worship their family idol. Prophet Mohammed knew that these personal idol Gods or Goddesses were the root cause of blood shed in the precincts of the holy shrine. Therefore it was pertinent as well as it was divinely ordained for him to throw away these idols and establish Tawhid the unity of Allah or the supreme Reality. This was the greatest revolution the prophet did in the pagan Arabia. It was the greatest religious, social, cultural and spiritual revolution which opened new horizons for the pagan Arabs. The concept of Tawhid brought all the Arabs together. Tawhid established unity of God as much as it established equality of all in the social religious, cultural and spiritual arena.

Islamic mysticism talks about two types of the vision of Allah :

> *"The vision of Allah is of two kinds; one seeing the manifestation of Allah's attributes of perfect beauty directly in the hereafter, and the other is seeing the manifestation of the divine attributes reflected upon the clear mirror of the pure heart, in this life, in this world. In such a case the manifestation of light emanating from the Perfect Beauty of Allah and is seen by the eye of the essence of the heart."*[14]

The Islamic mysticism that is Sufism stresses upon the three main principles which every salik in the path must have to adhere to. These principles are derived from the very word Tasawwuf. Alternatively the word Tasawwuf is consisted of the four letters T, S, W, F the main principles or in other sense the roots of Islamic mysticism. These four roots are as under.

1. Tawba (Repentence)
2. Safa (serenity)
3. Wilaya (Sainthood)
4. Fana fi Allah (Unity of Allah)

Tawba (Repentance) means feeling of regret and remorse for wrong-doing and turning towards Allah again with a new intention to make up for what one has neglected. According to truth-seeking scholars, repentance signifies a sincere effort to be saved from opposing the Divine Essence in feelings, thoughts, intentions and acts and to comply sincerely with His commands and prohibitions. Repentance does not consist in feeling disgust at something bad or prohibited and giving up doing it. Repentance is remaining aloof from whatever God hates and prohibits, even if it seems agreeable to sense and reasons.

The Qur'an says :

> *O you who believe! Turn to God in true, sincere repentance.*[15]

There are three categories of repentance :

(*a*) The first is the repentance of ordinary people who are unable to recognize Divine truths. A man feels his disobedience to God and, conscious of his sinfulness turns towards God and expresses his repentance with words–such as :

> *'Forgive me O God I have fallen or committed a sin, forgive me'!*

(*b*) The second is the repentance of those half-awakened to Divine truth : These are the people who are always conscious and are doing good and feeling omnipresence of God. If they commit any sinful deed then they immediately take refuge with the mercy and Favour of God. One with such degree of wakefulness and spiritual alertness is as described in the following tradition. Prophet Mohammed ﷺ declared :

> *One who sincerely repents of hi sin is as if he had never committed it. When God loves a servant of His, his sins do not harm him. Then he recited the verse : 'Assuredly, God loves the oft-repentant and those who always seek to purify themselves.'*

When asked about the sign of repentance, he declared : It is heart-felt remorse.

(c) The third one is of those who live so careful a life that, as is declared in a Tradition, even while they themselves are sleeping, their hearts are awake, immediately discard whatever intervenes between God and their hearts and other innermost faculties and regain the consciousness of their relation to the Light of the Lights. They always manifest the meaning of :

> *How excellent a servant! Truly he was ever turning in contrition (to his Lord). (38.44)*

Repentance means regaining one's essential purity after every spiritual deformation, and frequent self-renewal. The stages of repentance are :

- one feels sincere remorse and regret;
- one is frightened whenever one remembers the sins one has committed in the past;
- one tries to eradicate injustices and supports justice and right;
- one reviews one's responsibilities and performs or makes up obligations neglected in the past;
- one reforms oneself by removing spiritual defects caused by deviations and errors;
- one regrets and laments the ties one has spent without mentioning or remembering God and thinking Him and reflecting on his works, and is always apprehensive and alert that one's thoughts and feelings may be tainted by things that intervene between oneself and God. This last quality is particular especially to those greatly distinguished with nearness to God.

Mawlana Jalal al-Din al-Rumi says about sincere repentance :

I have repented and turned to God so sincerely
that I will not break [the vow of penitence] until my soul leaves my body.
In fact, who other than an ass steps towards perdition
after having suffered so much trouble
(on account of his sins)?[16]

The first station of an initiate in the path of mysticism is repentance, while the second is inaba (sincere atonement). In everyday usage, inaba is also used to express the ceremony held when a man submits himself to a spiritual guide (murshid). While repentance requires training feelings, thoughts and acts to direct them from opposition to admission and obedience, sincere penitence demands critique of the authenticity, sincerity and sufficiency of that admission and obedience. Repentance is a progressing or journeying toward God–meaning efforts to do whatever is pleasing to God and refraining from whatever is forbidden by Him. Sincere penitence is ascension through the stations of journeying in God-meaning efforts to live an upright life in self annihilation and in absorption to seek God's good pleasure in whatever one does and thinks. Awba (turning to God in contrition), is an ascension through the stations of journeying from God–meaning being responsible for guiding others after having embodied the Islamic way of mysticism, thought and conduct.

The words expressing repentance uttered by those who are always conscious of being in the omnipresence of God in fact express sincere penitence or turning to God in contribution. Prophet Mohammed ﷺ used to say I ask God's forgiveness seventy or a hundred times a day.

Safa or *Sakina* literally meaning calmness, silence, steadiness, solemnity, familiarity, subsidence of waves and tranquility. In the language of Sufism, Safa means that a heart becomes at rest by the gifts coming from the Unseen. Such a result heart is always in the expectation of the breezes to come from the realms beyond.

Safa sometimes comes in the form of signs perceptible or imperceptible, while at other times it appears so clearly that even ordinary people can identify it. Sometimes Safa and the signs of it are of the kind of some spiritual breaths or Divine breezes which can only be perceived with great care. Or, at other times, they come miraculously and as clearly as, or in such manifest forms that, everyone can see. The ranks or stations called 'ridaya' (being pleased with God in resignation) and 'mardiyya' (being approved by God) are two dimensions of peacefulness belonging to the good and virtuous and depths of resignation. The ranks called 'mulhama' (being inspired by God) and 'zakiyya' (being purified by God) are two other degrees of peacefulness relating to those brought near to God which are difficult to perceive and the gifts that come through them are pure and abundant.

All these four roots combined with the other as discussed in detail in chapter 3 Tasawwuf leads to the Realization of Allah. The Sharia people do not recognise all these roots as they separate the Supreme self as distinct from the Self or the Atman as described by the Upanishads. There is a concept in the religion of Islam as a separate creator of the world. Allah according to Islam created the phenomenal world and he is the sole person sovereign and Supreme hence none but only Allah should be worshipped. The Holy Quran says that there should not be any partner in the worship except the Allah.

Sufi's are Muslim mystics who trace their spiritual lineage to the great Prophet Mohammad, the founder of Islam. Like all mystics, Sufi's are not concerned with second hand knowledge about God, but with personal experience of God.

For Sufis, the outer forms of religion are merely vehicles for the spiritual content that lies beyond all rites and creeds. The Sufi sage Shibli is said to have run the streets carrying flaming coals announcing he was going to set fire to the Ka'aba, the most sacred place, in Islam, so that Muslims would concern themselves less with a place and more with the Lord of the Ka'ba. Such enthusiasm for truth has often caused Sufis to be branded as heretics, and horribly persecuted by orthodox islamic authorities. Yet their wisdom has survived to inspire generations of spiritual seekers.

Sufism is a voyage of discovery into ourselves and beyond ourselves; a pilgrimage to become perfect servants of Allah; a love affair with the Divine Beloved in which the lovers merge in mystical union. The Sufis may seem esoteric and mystifying but actually they are trying to point us to something so obvious that we miss it.

God is everywhere and everything. We are God. There is nothing but the oneness of God. It is only our sense of being a separate ego that obscures the omnipresent Truth.

Sufism is simply about seeing things as they truly are–a mystical realization tht is available to all.

When the Sufi saint Rabi'a heard Salih of Qazwin teaching "Knock and the Door will open for you" she admonished him. "What are you talking about Salih; the Door has never been shut."

The Sufis approach God through many divine Names that express his various attributes but the Name "Allah" combines and transcends all these attributes, Allah is the Supreme Reality. The world Allah combines the roots "al" and "la" to express "The Oneness of Being and Nothingness."

God embraces all opposites. As it says in the Holy Qu'ran "He is the first and the last, the apparent and the hidden." He is the "Soul of all souls", as Rumi puts it. He is not confined by any one creed but is the one God who speaks through all genuine religion, manifesting himself in different ways appropriate to the individual seeker.

The mystical aspects of the Vedanta and Sufism have much in common because both the currents (Shari'a and tariqa) lead to the Supreme Reality. The methods of realization suggested by both the currents may differ but they differ in degree not in kind. The self as lauded by the Upanishads is none else but the Isme Azam of Sufism. The Hallajian passion for the Supreme Reality reflected into Sufism and particularly the words (An-al Haq) uttered by Mansur AL-Hallaj seem to be inspired by the Vendanta.

The Sufis did not visit India and they did have contact with the Upanishadic seers. The history of mankind has much to tell us about the valued treasure of our past which even the seers and the mystics of the foreign land took benefit for the uplift of mankind.

Whatever be the roots of Sufism and the Vendanta, they unanimously herald the unity of the soul with the Supreme Reality. The concept of Tawhid merged with the utterance of Mansur with his An-al-Haq tempts us to see 'Sarvam khalu idam Brahman' and let us to realize 'Aham Brahmasmi'. When one realizes the Supreme Reality his outer garments of the rituals and religious sects drop automatically. The need of the day is to see the Reality in its magnanimity and to see the religion in its nakedness. The need of the day is to understand the spiritual aspects of Religions and to have a taste of the nectar. What had happened to Manur and Janak, and Astvakra and Buddha and Mahavir and Ain-al-Qudat-al-Hamdhani and Sarmad and Kabir and nanak and Tulsi and Rahim and Rabi'a and Meera can also happen to us. But do we deserve it? Certainly we do deserve, for the Upanishads say that the Self and the Brahman are the one and the same. The Sufis also beat the same drum. Then where does discordance lie? The discordance lie in the ignorance in the words of Shankara the discordance lies in 'Avidya' or 'Maya'. This is true of phenomenal world as well as spiritual world. Discordance or conflict among the people of different Religions is the outcome of ignorance. They miss the point where the Ultimate Reality becomes one. The common Hindus miss the point and the Muslim remain stuck to Sharia. This Avidya or ignorance or false knowledge must be removed and the Truth need be realized. Only then we can build one world, one humanity, one Religion-the Religion of Truth and humanity or the Religion of the Self and the Super Self. The Truth is the same and shall remain the same without any effect of time and place. This Truth is the Truth of the 'Brahman' in the Upanishadic language and 'Haq' in the Sufistic language. I would like to sum up by a beautiful yet potent mantra from the Upanishads :

Yasmin sarvani bhutani atmaivabhud vijanatah
Tatra ko mohah kah shokah ekatvam nupasyatah[17]

When one realizes the Supreme Reality there never remains any delusion or sorrow for him. The one who has realized the Brahman becomes unaffected by phenomenal or wordly things. This is the glory of the upanishads and this is the pulchritude of Sufism. This is the mystery of the Vedanta and secret of Sufism which falls in the forms of blessings upon the mystics in the language of Pustimarga it is the Pusti Varsha (Shower of Blessings) on the seers.

References

1. Satyam jnanam anatam Brahma, Taittiriya Upanishad Brahamanandvalli.
2. sarvam hi etad brahma, ayamatma brahma. Mandukya Upanishad 2-7.

   Jivo brahmaiva naparaha Shankaracharya. Brahmajnanavalimala-20.
3. Katha Upanishad. III, 12.
4. yathagneh ksudra visphlinga vyuccaranti eameva asmad atmanah sarve pranah, sarve lokah, sarve devah, sarvani, bhutani vyuccaranti. Brihadaranayaka Upanisha. II.I.20.
5. Mundaka Upanishad. II.II.11.
6. Asato ma sadgmaya. Tamaso ma jyotirgamaya. Mrutyur ma amrutamgamaya.
7. sasyamiva martyah pachyate sasyamiva jayate punah. Katha Upanishad I.I.6.
8. Atma va idam eka evaagra asit, nanyat kin cana misat sa aiksata lokan nu sruja iti Aitareya Upanisad Verse I.
9. *Brihadaranyak Upanishad 4.4.*
10. *Brihadaranyak Upanishad 4.5.*
11. Ibn-al Arabi Fusus-al Hikam.
12. Ibn-al Arabi Fusus-al Hikam.
13. Dr. Yajneshar Shastri Lecture on "Islamic mysticism" University of Cleveland Ohio.
14. The Secret of the Secrets Hadrat Abdul Qadir Jilani.
15. Quran Sura 66 verse 8.
16. Mathnavi Rumi Translated by R.A. Nicholson.
17. Ishavasya Upanishad.

Glossary of Sufi Terms[1]

1. ADAB

A-dab

Manners, in this case, the manners of the dervish. It is said that the whole art of being a dervish is in one's manners, not only how one treats God, but even more, in how one treats one's fellow humans. The traditional dervishes have many beautiful rituals entwined with every aspect of daily life, especially in greeting and being with each other, which help to maintain awareness of the Divine presence.

2. ALHAMDDULILLAH

al-hamdu-li- *'Liah.*

"Praise for God." (There is no such word in Arabic as "Alhamdu*lee*lah.")

3. ALLAAHU AKBAR

al-*llahu ak*-bar. (In Persian the u becomes an o, so we get "Allaho Akbar")

Lit., "God is the Most Great."

4. ASSTA'FIRU'LLAH

as-tah-fir-u-'Llah (Turkish pronunciation of the Arabic as-tagh-firu 'Llah. The "gh" sound just sort of goes away in Turrkish.)

Lit., "I ask God's forgiveness." From the same root as Ghafoor, the "All-Forgiving," a Divine Name, Due to the emotional loading mot of us have on the concept of 'forgiveness," the concentration "I take refuge in Allah" might be more useful.

5. BARAKA

ba-ra-ka. pl. or intensified, "barakat."

The transformative blessing power, or the transformative presence of a teacher.

6. BAYAT

ba-yat.

Initiation; the acceptance of a student into a holy Order–the linking of the being of the student with that of the teacher and with the Chain of Transmission of the Esoteric School and the Spiritual Hierarchy, where the teacher assumes a certain responsibility of the student and the student reaffirms the pledge made by the soul in pre-eternity dedicating itself to becoming an instrument for the transfiguration of the world.

7. BISMI 'LLAH IR'RAHMAN IE-RAHIM

bi-smi-'Lllllllah-i ra'hman-i ra'heem.

Lit., 'With the Name of God, the Beneficent, the Merciful." This invocation begins every day, every undertaking, and indeed, every act of the Sufi, for there are no "ordinary" acts–only sacred acts and unconscious acts.

8. CHERAG

sher-ag (from Persian, tchir-agh, "a lamp.") Cherags are lighted on the tombs of the Peers on particular occasion or every evening.

9. DERVISH

(From Persian, dar-veesh, into Arabic, dar-weesh; Lt., "threshold" or "doorstill")

Originally a reference to the experience of opening the door in the morning to find a way in a patched cloak camped in the recessed doorway of your house. Means, variously and according to context, an initiate of a Sufi school, one such possessing a particularly uncompromising attitude toward Truth, or someone having crossed the threshold of enlightenment.

9. DOWA

du-aa.

Lit., "supplication." A term in Islam for non-obligatory prayers. Also the "title" (see Annotation, "Prayers") Seeking of blessings of God through Peer.

10. ELEMENT BREATHS

Also called the purification Breaths, or sometimes incorrectly, the "healing breaths." This is a concentration on the breath in which one absorbs one's consciousness into the "elements" of earth, water, fire, air, and ether, each in turn.

11. FANA, FANA-FI

fa-na, faaa-na-fee

Absorption or effacement into a being or attribute. The grades are traditionally listed as Fana-fi-Shaikh (effacement in one's teacher), Fana-fi-Rasul (effacement in the prophet), Fana-fi-'Llah (fa-na-fee 'Llah) (effacement in God). The master of this process is said to be in a condition of Baqa', "subsistence" in the Divine.

12. FAQIR

faa-qeer

(Lit., "poor one," connoting poor in personal ego. Pl., fuqara.) Another word for "dervish," especially in North Africa.

13. FIKR

fikr. (Lit., "contemplation.") The linking of a Divine name with the breath. The "Fikr ass'Sirr" (sirr means "mystery' or secret") is the formless contemplation upon or absorption into the essence of the Name.

14. GATHA

Properly, ga-ta, san-ga-ta. "Gatha" is the Avestan (old Persian) word for "song".

15. HAL (haal)

Lit., "state" or "condition.") A special-purpose, temporary

state of consciousness, generally a product of spiritual practices. A hal (pl. "awhal") is by nature gratuitous and one should not attempt to prolong it. For every true hal (and there are test for this, part of the " 'llm-i-Awhal, " the "Science of States"), there is a counterfeit of it based on personal emotion and fantasy.

16. HAZRAT/HAD-RAT

haz-rat (Persian, from Arabic, had-rat)

"The Presence." This is an honorific, generally given to great teachers who have passed away from the earth. In proper usage, this proceeds designations of rank and title.

17. HU

hoo. (this is not the "aspirated" h)

(Arabic. This word is gender-nonspecific, meaning equally "he" and "she") The living presence of God.

18. INAYAT

'i-naa-yat khan refers to the name of a person

("Inayat" means "lucky" or "thoroughly conscientious.")

19. INSAN AL-KAAAMIL

in-saan al-kameel.

The perfected human being.

20. INSHA'LLAH

in-shaa-'llah

"If God so wills."

21. ISHQ ALLAH MA'ABUD LILLAM

'Ishq al-llah ma-'a-bood lee-llah. (Note that ma 'abud has three syllables) ("Lillah" & "Ma'abud.")

Lit., "The love of God is adored by that which is divine." Freely translated as "God is love, the Lover, and the beloved."

"Tis God Who is the one loved in every beloved one, and it is God Who loves through each lover the infinite reflections of the attributes of the Divine perfection." ibn al "Arabi.

22. JELAL

ja-lal

(Lit., "power" or "grandeur.") Things or energies in their active or explicitly commanding phase, more or less. (There is no accurate verbal definition for this quality. It does not equate with "male" or "yang," though the flavour of this energy is in some ways similar.)

23. JEMAL

ja-mal

(Lit., "beauty" or "devotion.") Things or energies in their receptive phase. (Again more or less equally hard to define. It does not equate with "female" or "yin" though feels somewhat similar.)

24. KEMAL

ka-mal

(Lit., "perfection.") Things in their absorbed, effaced, or disintegrated phase.

25. KHALIF(A)

Kha-leef.

A direct representative of a teaching master of the Sufis (termed Sheikh or Murshid, depending on local usage). In the system of initiations once used in the Sufi Order, this was equivalent in level to Shaikh.

26. KHATUM

properly, kha-tum

(Lit., "the closing recital" or "to place a seal.") The closing prayer, recited at the close of classes and ceremonies in the Sufi schools.

In ordinary life it also means offerings made in memory of the dead of reciting the Quran and offering sweets.

27. LA ILAHA ILLA 'LLAH

la-i-la-ha 'il-la 'Llah. (This does not get the "aspirated" h)

The correct pronunciation of the last syllables is " illa 'llah," not "ill Aallah."

Exoterically, "There is no God but Allah," esoterically, it means something like 'There is no reality except the essential unity of all things, beings, and consciousness."

28. MAJDDDHUB

Ar., maj-dhoob, pers. maj-zoob

Lit., "Insane," "possessed," "magnetically attracted." In this content it means a "God-intoxicated" holy man. The spelling "madhzub" is an Anglicization of the Persian pronunciation.

29. MALAMA, MALAMATI

ma-la-maa, ma-la-ma-ti.

A designation for certain dervishes who cultivate the reprobation of the conventional social sphere. Sufism has been called the path of blasphemy particularly by the people on the Shari's.

30. MAQAM

ma-qam

(Lit., :station.") One's spiritual station or developmental stage, as distinct from one's hal, or state of realization. This is seen as the outcome of one's effort to transform oneself, whereas the hal is a gift. "Maqam" is also a term for "scale" or "mode" in Near Eastern music especially Divine.

31. MASHAIKH

ma-shaikh.

(Means something like "Elder among Shaikhs.") In the old system of initiations in the Sufi order, a rank equivalent to murshid. "Shaikh ul-Masshaik" is a rank equivalent to Pir-o-Murshid.

32. MASHALLAH

maa-shaa-'Llah. Loosely, "'Tis God who has done it!" Equivalent to Alhamdu-Lillah.

33. MEVLANA

mev-la-na. Americanization of Persian, mev-la-na and Arabic, maw-la-na or Indian maulana literally our master.

Usually referring to Mevlana Jelauddin Rumi, the Sufi master in whose name the Mevlevi (mev-lev-i or mevlevi) Order was founded. This order is known as the Whirling Dervish order.

34. MOHAMMED AR-RASULU'LLAH

mo-ham-med ar-ra-sool-u 'Llah.

(Litd., "The Praiseworthy One is the Prophet of God.") Esoterically, an attunement to, or invocation of the prototype of the Perfected human in the world of form.

35. MUREED

mu-reed. (not myoo-reed.")

A student in a Sufi school.

36. MURSHID

mur-shid

A most senior teacher in a Sufi school. The feminine is "murshida." Related by the root R-Sh-D to "ar-Rassshid," "The Unerring," a Divine Name.

37. NABI

na-bee.

Aa variety of prophet, traditionally a notch in "rnk" below Rasul; the giver of a Message to a specific community rather than a world Message.

38. NAFS

Nafs means both "ego" and "breath." Traditionally, Sufi training takes a student through seven stages of refinement of the ego (termed the "seven men"), from the most unconscious and trained to the most transparent-to-the-Divine. Nafs refers to the baser or lower instinct.

39. NAYAZ

na-yaz.

The healing invocation.

40. NAZAR

na-zr, Persian pronunciation of Arabic "na-dhar," Equal accent on the syllables.

(Lit., "a beneficent glance.") The blessing prayer on sustenance.

41. NUZUL

nu-zool

(Litd., "setting" or "descending.") The settling or expelling of things, especially the current of breath. Related by the roof N-Z-L to "Manzil," meaning "waystation" or "stopping place. 'URUJ. Spelled Nasul in some older editions of the Esoteeric literature.

42. ORDER(S)

The Sufi "Orders," called such in the West due to an imagined parallel with the Christians monastic orders, are really initiatic lineages. The Sufi equivalent term is "tarrriqat" and refers to the initiatic unity of the past and present members of the school, and the particular flavor of the attunement and technical specialization of the lineage. The Sufi tariqats are not organizations. "Sufi organization" is a contradiction in terms, being that a distinctive characteristic of the Ssufi Way is the emphasis on inner realities instead of external forms.

There are four major lineages or Silsilas : the Qadiri, Suhrawardi, Chishti, and the Naqshbandi (which is the present day visible expression of the original, Source tradition, called in earlier times the Khwajajan), and numerous off schools and branches of these, such as the halveti, mevlevi Bektashi, Rifa'i, etc.

43. PIR/peer

(From Persian, "Old man.") The founder or head of a Sufi

school or lineage. “Pir-o-Murshid” means “Elder and Guide.” The prayer by

44. QASAB

qa-sab

(Lit., “tubes” or “channels.”) The Sufi alternate-nostril breathing practice, of which there are numerous forms for different purposes. Spelled Kasab in some older editions of the Esoteric Papers.

45. RASUL

ra-sool.

A major prophet, the giver of a Message to the whole of humanity. The prayer by this name is usually recited by Sufis, Rsul refers only to the prophet of Islam Mohmmedﷺ.

46. RUH

rooh. (Note the “aspirated” h.), pl. ar-wah

Means “breath of life,” “soul,” “spirit.” Ruh al-Quddus = The Holy Spirit.

47. AS-SALAAAAM-O-ALAAYKUM

sa-laam a-lay-kum

“Peace be with (or upon) thee.” The appropriate response is “Wa’lay-kum Salaam :” “And upon thou, Peace.” It is incumbent upon Muslims to greet each other thus, and greeting a Muslim in this way implies you are one, too. Be careful.

48. SALAT

saa-lat

Lit., “prayer.” This word in Islam refers to the formal obligatory prayers.

49. SAMA

sa-maa.

Lit., “hearing”, related by root to “same”, “to hear”).

The sacred assembly of the dervishes, originally for the purpose of listening to consciousness-expanding music, under the guidance of and in rapport with a sheikh)in which, incidentally, the dervishes were required to remain absolutely still for the duration of the exercise). This term was later extended to include listening to and reciting mantric poetry, and in the Mevlevi tradition, the performance of the whirling meditation known as "The Turning".

50. SAUM (sa-*oom*).

(From a Persian word meaning "opening recital", from the same root as *sama*). In the lineage founded by Inayat Khan, the *prayer* designed thus is recited at dawn, and at the opening of the formal class gatherings in which the Esoteric Papers are read. (Please note the pronunciation : Emphasis on the last syllable; the way most folks inflect this, they say "to make a fast", or sometimes, "poison").

51. SHAGHAL (*sha*-ghal)

(Lit., "absorption" or "preoccupation"). The name of an advanced breath/energy practice.

52. SHAIKH (Shakh)

"Elder". In this context, a senior teacher in a Sufi school. The feminine is "shaikha".

53. SILSILA (sil-sil-a)

(Lit., "chain or pedigree). The "Chain of Transmission" or initiatic lineage of the Masters of a Sufi school.

54. SUBHAN ALLAH (sub-*han* a-*Llah*)

Lit., 'Glory be to God!', "God is Purity" is not really a correct translation, but it does aim one in a useful emotional direction. This phrase is usually given as a practice of purification, but is ultimately a *zikr* of glorification.

55. SUFI (*soo-fee*)

There are numerous theories on the origin of this word, including Soof ("wool"), Sophos (Greek, "wisdom"), Saaf ("purity"), Sofa ("the People of the Bench"), and others. Al-Hujwiri, a very great teacher in India, has stated that the word itself has mantric value but is an invented word with no etymologyṭSoof, Sophos, Saaf, and so forth being synchronously associated but not its origin. In some places, the Sufi's woolen cloak (worn for qualities of magnetism inherent in undyed wool) became an identifying symbol or badge. (One never claims oneself to be a Sufi, as the word connotes attainment).

56. TASAWWUF (ta-sa-*woof*)

Literally, "the doing of the Sufi Way", or "that which emerges from the being of the Sufi". The traditional Sufi term for what we call "sufism". Associated by the root **TS-W-F** with "Sufi". The word is derived from t, zs, w and f. These letters suggest the inner musicality of the word that is denoted by all these letters separately as :

T means **Tawba** *i.e., repentence*

S means **Safa** or **Safina** *i.e.,* serenity, modesty and humility in the way.

W means **Wasl** or the union with supreme Reality.

F means **Fana**, which is the end goal of Islamic Mysticism. Fana means to become one with the Supreme reality.

57. TASAWWURI (ta-sa-*woo-ree*)

The forming of an image in creative imagination. From the same **S-W-R** root as MUSAWWIR, "the Fashioner", a Divine Name. One of the defining practices of the Sufi way is **"Tasawwuri Murshid",** or "living inwardly in the manner of the Master", in which one progresses from acting out a created image of the Murshid (to experiencing one self being "overlaid" by and then absorbed into the living presence of the Murshid. One's condition at this point is termed "**Tawajjuh**" (ta-wa-*jjuh*, "possessing the countenance", not to be confused with the word 'tawajid'), and is equivalent to **Fana-fi-Shaikh.**

58. TASBIH (tass-bih, "Tass-bi", is OK, but not "taz-bi")

The Sufi rosary or "prayer beads". Also called "misbaha".

Tasbih also means "the act of glorifying God" (or invoking sacred names on one's rosary) and comes from the same **s-b-h** root as "**s**ub**h**an".

59. TAWHID

taw-***heed*** (Lit., "union")

The Testament of Unity, especially the phrase "**La ilaha illa 'LIAH**". Related by root (**W-H-D**) to "*waah*id" ("numeral one", and al-Waa**h**id, a Divine Name), "wa**h***eed*" ("unique"), "wa**h**dan*iyyat*" ("the solitude of the Divine Unity") and "A**h**ad" (absolute oneness)

60. URUJ

{u-*roodj.*

The rising wave or waxing or expanding of things, especially the current of the breath.

61. URS

oorss (not "erz")

Lit., "wedding". The passing of a Sufi Saint, seen as the ultimate unification with God the Beloved; also, the anniversary of same. The urs of the founder and of great saints of a pedigree are traditionally times of celebration by the members of that school.

62. WAZIFE

wa-zee-**fa** (wa-*zee*-fa is acceptable. The plural is "wa-za-*eef*")

Lit., "occupation " or "duty". The Sufi power words, akin to the mantra of other traditions. Most, but not all, of the wazifas are drawn from what in formal Islam are called the "Ninety-nine Most Beautiful Names of Allah". In metaphysical terms they can be seen as "phone numbers" to the basic energies that run the universe. In psychological terms, these energies are the pure forms of which the various aspects of the human personality are distorted concretizations.

63. YA (yaa)

An invocation, something like "O Thou!"

YA SHAFFEE, YA KAFFEE

shaa-ffee, equally accented.

(Lit., "O Healer, O All-Sufficient"). The healing wazifas. We have been taught that Ya Kaffee means "O Remedy", but "All-Sufficient" is a more accurate translation. (Also note that, using the standard transliteration scheme, the spelling "Khaffee", with a **kh**, changes the meaning to "hidden")

64. ZIKR

zikr, pronounced in Arabic something like "thikr" (**th** as in 'this') and "zikr" in Persian and non-Arabic-speaking countries.

(Lit., "rememberance"). The practice of remembering (or recovering our knowledge of) of the unity of things. Strictly speaking, this refers to group or individual practices such as repeating **wazifas** and the tawid, but is most generally used to mean just the tawhid. See **LA ILAHA 'ILLA' LLAH** and **TAWHID**. There are many, many forms of the practice; each of the Orders has their characteristic zikr, and there are variations for special purposes. There are forms repeated silently, there are some done aloud, and there are some sung and/or done standing and/or moving in specific patterns, called "ha**d**rat" or "zikr iqyam".

Explanation

LA ELLAHA EL IL ALLAH HŬ Despite its acceptance through usage and reverence for the transmission of a certain teacher, this particular attempt at the pronunciation of the tawhid is not coherent as language, is rhythmically inharmonious, and has other problems.

'There are...distinct aspects of Zikr which must be made clear before a mureed, for each of these... aspects has its distinct and definite work to perform in the evolution of a mureed. The first aspect is the clear and correct repetition of the Zikr : La ilaha illa llahu, which but be repeated without taking a breath between. Every word must be pronounced distinctly, rhythmically, and in onebreath."

LILLAH Li-llah, accent always on the last syllable. There is a tendency of English speakers to say "laylah," s in "Rasul laylah." Laylah is a perfectly good Arabic word, but it means "night time." It is Ra-sul-u-'Llah, or ma-'a-bood li-llah.

MA'ABUD There are two similar sounding words, "ma'abud and 'maboob." They come from different roots. ma'abud means, "adored one," "the one to whom I am enslaved by my love," and is related by root to the word" "abdd," "servant" or "slave." Mahboob is a variation on "abib," "beloved one." (Using standard transliteration, there is no word in Arabic sounding like "Mahbud," since "h" is always pronounced.)

ORIGIN The origin of the Sufi way is a mystery itself. Most Islamic Sufis trace the origins of the path to the prophet mohammed, at least when speaking in public There is, however, a tradition amongst some elements of the naqshbandi order that, inasmuch as the basis of the Sufi Way is inherent in the structure of the human being and of consciousness, it has existed in all times and place, regardless of outward forms; it is actually essence of the various streams of inspiration transmitted by each of the prophets. The Naqshbandis claim the historical origins of the Sufi way to be 40,000 years old.

PRAYERS A careful reading of the universal Worship manual shows that, in the Universal Worships service at least, the words Saum, Salat, and Khatum are never referred to as the "titles" of these prayers, but more like labels for a particular stage of process. It may therefore be somewhat incorrect to refer to "the prayer Saum," and we definitely risk offending Muslims by saying "the Prayer Salat."

ROSE Beads used for counting prayers originated with the Hindus, and were retained by the Buddhists. The Arabs adopted them from the Buddhists of eastern Persia, which was predominately Buddhist at the time of the Arab expansion. The Christians got them from the Saracens, part of the esoteric crosspollination going on at the tie. In Arabic, the word for "rose" (ward) is just a vowel away and related by root to the word for "invocation of sacred Names" (wird). Thus the rose symbolism in the Sufi way (connoting remembrance), and the name of this device in Christinanity : "Rosary."

Reference

1. The Glossary of Sufi Terms is compiled from various Urdu/ Persian and Arabic Sources particularly from those who are conversant with the Sufi terms. Acknowledgement is also made to the work of Peer Inayat Khan a Sufi.

Bibliography

(1) Shuja Alhaq : A Forgotten Vision, Vikas Publishing House Pvt. Ltd., Vol. 1, 1977.

(2) John A Subhan : Sufism Its Saints and Shrines, Cosmo Publications, Vol. 11-1999.

(3) H.A.Rose : Religious History of Islam, Amar Prakashan Delhi-1984.

(4) Sadhu Santideva : Introduction to Indian Mysticism, Cosmo Publications, India, 2000.

(5) Sadhu Santideva : Escetic Mysticism, Cosmo Publication, India, 2000.

(6) Karen Armstrong : Islam A Short History, A Modern Library Chronicles Book, New York, 2002.

(7) R.P. Masani : Persian Mysticism, Award Publishing House, New Delhi, 1981.

(9) Eknath Easwaran : The Upanishads, Penguin Books, 1987.

(10) Nagendra Kumar Singh : Islamic Mysticism in India, A.P.H. Publishing Corporation, New Delhi, 1996.

(11) Andrew Harvey : Love's Glory–recreation of Rumi, Viking Penguin Books, India, 2002.

(12) S.N. Dasgupta : Hindu Mysticism six lectures, Allied Publishers Pvt. Ltd., Bombay.

(13) Sadananda Yogendra : The Philosophy of the Vendanta and Vedantasara Translated by Paul Deussen and G.A. Jaccob, Bharatiya Publishing House, Delhi, 1979.

(14) Muarice Bucaille : The Bible The Quran and Science Kazi Publication, Lahore, 1976.

(15) Frederick Mathewson Denny : An Introduction to Islam Macmillan Publishing Co., New York, 1994.

(16) Robert Earnest Hume : The Thirteen Principal Upanishads, Oxford University Press, Delhi, 1949.

(17) David Waines : An Introduction to Islam, Cambridge University Press, 1995.

(18) S. Radhakrishnan : The Principal Upanishads, Harper Collins Publishers, India, 1994.

(19) A.J. Arberry : A Sufi martyr, Georege Allen and Unwin Ltd., London, 1969.

(20) J.H.M. Whiteman : The Mystical Life Faber and Faber, London, 1961.

(22) Holy Bible : The catholic Edition for India, Thomas Nelson, Bangalore, 1001.

(22) Warner : The Yogi and The Mystic, Curzon Press, Surrey, 1989.

(23) Rumi : The Hidden Music, Translated by Azima Melita Kolin and Maryam Mạfi, Thorsons, 2001

(24) Richard Woods : Understanding Mysticism, The Athelon Press, London, 1980.

(25) Anwar Kazi : Anwar kavya (Gujarati), Millennium Prakashan Shree Harihar Pustakalaya Surat, 1954.

(26) Yajneshwar S Shastri (Dr.) Foundations of Hinduism, Yogeshewar Prakashan, Ahmedabad, 1993.

(27) Carl W. Earnest : Sufism, Shambhala South Asia Edition, 2000.

(28) Religions of the World, St. Martins Press New York, 1993, Edited Volume.

(29) Akbar S Ahmed : Post Modernism and Islam, Penguin Books, 1995.

(30) R A Nicholson : Studies in Islamic Mysticism Adam Publishers and Distributors, Delhi, 1998.

(31) Seyyed Hossein Nasr : Islamic Spirituality, SCM Press Ltd., London, 1991.

(32) A J Arberry : An Account of the Mystics of Islam, Mandala Unwin Paperbacks, London, 1979.

(33) Thomas Cleary : The Essential Koran, Harper Collins Publishers India, 1994.

(34) W Stoddart and R A Nicholson : Sufism Adam Publishers, Delhi, 1998.

(35) Gwilyam Beckerlegge : The World Religions Reader Routledge, London, 1998.

(36) A Yusuf Ali : The Holy quran, Amana Corporation Maryland, 1983.

(37) Manudev Bandhu : Chhandogya Upanishad (Hindi) Chukhamba Series, Varanasi, 1967.

(38) Shiv Narain Shastri : Ishopanishad Bhasya (Hindi) Chaukhamba Series, Varansi, 1967.

(39) S A H Abidi : Sufism in India, Wishwa Prakashan, New Delhi, 1992.

(40) Muhammad Ibn-Al-Husayn-Al-Sulami : The Book of Sufi Chivalry East west Publication London and The Hague, 1983. Translation-Sheikh Yosun Bayrak al-halveti.

(41) Fariduddin Attar : The Conference of the Birds, Translation-C S Nott, Routledge & Kegan Paul Ltd., London, 1954.

(42) Hadrat Abdul Qadir Al-Jilani : The Secret of the Secrets. The Islamic Texts Society, UK, 1992.

(43) Robert A Thurman : the Tibetan Book of the Dead, Harper Collins Publishers, India, 2001.

(44) Muhyiddin Shakoor : The writing on the Water Element Books Dorset, 1987.

(45) Fariduudin Attar : The Muslim Saints and Mystics, Translation A J Arberry, Arkan Penguin, 1990.

(46) Yajneshwar S Shastri (Dr.) : The Mayhanasutralankara of Asanga–A Study in Vijnanvadabuddhism. Sri Satlguru Publication, Delhi, 1989.

(47) William Loftus Hare : Mysticism of East and West Routledge and Legan Paul, London, 1964.

(48) Margaret Smith : Rabia Basri the mystic and her fellow Saints Faber and Faber, London, 1967.

(49) Andrew Harcvey : The Teachings of Rumi, Shambhala South Asian Edition, 2000.

(50) Ali Bin Uthman Al-Hujwiri : The Kash Al Mahjub Translation R A Nicholson Taj Company, New Delhi, 1999.

(51) Shri Vasudev Mahashankar Joshi : Taittiriya Upanishad (Gujarati) with commentary and Shankara Bhasya Sasltu Sahitya Vardhak Karyalaya Ahmedabad, 1978.

(52) Acharya Rajneesh : Sufis–The People of the Path Vol. I & II, Rajneesh Ashram Pune, 1986.

Index